Marketing That Really Works

Marketing That Really Works

How to Build #1 Brands Fast

Darren C Contardo

Host of The Marketer's Commute Podcast
&
Author of The Marketer's Commute
"How To" eBook Series

THE MARKETER'S
COMMUTE

www.MarketingThatReallyWorks.net
www.TheMarketersCommute.com/book
www.darrencontardo.net/book

ISBN: 0692781560
ISBN 13: 9780692781562

Dedication

To my beautiful wife Steph and incredible sons Van and Gunnar. You are the purpose in my life that I didn't know existed earlier. For those who have helped me learn and grow over the years, thank you. I hope this book does you justice.

Table of Contents

Introduction

Marketing. What exactly is it, and why does everyone think they can do it? Well, the answer is simple; marketing is the art and science of creating needs from wants and delivering meaningful value for the goods or services. And since we are all consumers most people feel they are qualified to do marketing. The truth is you absolutely are qualified, but like all things, with experience, study, a curious mind, and a lot of trial and error you can become much more efficient and effective at creating marketing strategies that really work, saving yourself headaches, second guessing, third-party criticisms, and of course money.

I have been doing marketing now for 22 years, or somewhere in the area of 45,000 hours. During those years, months, weeks, and hours I have made A LOT of mistakes. Looking back now I could have avoided those wrong turns if I searched out the right information; of course, some of those mistakes only made me sharper, smarter, and a better marketer. This is my mission for you: I want you to be a genius marketer! To leap-frog over average, pitfalls, and wasted time or money. I want you to create powerful marketing strategies that work time and time again, creating real value for you and your customers.

"I have been doing marketing now for 22 years, or somewhere in the area of 45,000 hours. During those years, months, and hours I have made A LOT of mistakes… those mistakes only made me sharper."

So what is the blueprint for success? What is the magical formula? Well unfortunately there isn't a one-size-fits-all because "it depends." Ambiguity is always with us as marketers and, well, it's time for you to get you used to it. It depends on your company lifecycle, your budget, your industry, your target market, your product or service, and, honestly, what you're good at. However, here is the good news: In this book I'm going to share strategies, tactics, and principles that have helped me create multiple #1 brands in Canada, the U.K., The United States, and the world over. I haven't done this once, twice, or three times, but have had the luxury and opportunity to work with brilliant people who helped to create 16 top-selling brands in the health and wellness space in the world's top retailers.

"I have had the luxury and opportunity to work with brilliant people who helped to create 16 top-selling brands in the health and wellness space in the world's top retailers."

Just recently I've put my focus on consulting on pause and joined a team to turn the brand SlimFast around. SlimFast, once the largest weight-loss brand in the world, over the last 10 years declined every year losing nearly 90% of its sales. One of the top CPG multi-nationals was running with it and had nearly a dozen brand managers on it, but just could not get the brand going again. As a result it was sold to a private equity team in hopes they could do something. They restructured the internal team and also brought me on. By leading the marketing team, agencies, and other strategic partners we've managed to turn the brand around in 18 months and are now #1 again in both Canada and the United States. What did we do? We used many of the strategies I've laid out in this book to take a brand that was in free fall, reposition it, add some relevance, launch new products, increase distribution, and rework the entire marketing plan. Of course it's an incredible team effort and it took the trust, vision, and drive of an incredible CEO, Private Equity Team, and incredibly talented co-workers who are all rock stars!

In this book you'll learn the strategies, tactics, and processes that were used to turn around SlimFast and that I used to build 16 other #1 best-selling brands; you'll learn how to position your brand to make the competition irrelevant, how to set up your business, win on Amazon, capitalize on free marketing, use social media to drive email growth, buy media efficiently, how to measure success, and of course how to build your brand into #1 status!

> *"In this book you'll learn... how to build your brand into #1 status."*

You can do it, you really can. If you put in the work with the knowledge shared here you can be well on your way to becoming a marketing leader.

To learn more about marketing strategies or get even more insight visit darrencontardo.net or my podcast website at themarketerscommute.com. You can also listen to my The Marketer's Commute podcast on iTunes.

Yours Truly,

Darren "Giving Away all my Secrets" Contardo

Section 1

Do You Have What it Takes?

Chapter 1

How To Start a Business

You may have started your business already, or you may be thinking about starting your own business. Maybe you're asking yourself, "What are the steps that I should take in order to be successful?"

It can be done many different ways, but I think the big thing to really understand before you actually spend any money is the research. You can go into something and waste a lot of money and time if you don't have the right market, if you don't have the right product, and you really want to make those things right. It's the right opportunity, the timing and the market are right, there's demand, all those things are in place and clear.

Then the next most important question to ask yourself is "Do I have enough money to support it?" Is it something new that you have to spend a lot of money to educate people on what it is? Or is this a commodity, which requires just a little bit of a lower price point, or better packaging, or something like that? All these things are important.

> *"Before you actually spend any money, do the research… have the right market… the right product… and timing. Do you have to educate and spend lots of money or is it a commodity, which requires a lower price point or better packaging?"*

The reason why I'm bringing it up is because I've started many small businesses in the past and even larger ones. One of the things that I'd started – my first legitimate business – was selling travel. It was a multi-level marketing business. I was 18 years old, I did that for a while and I didn't sell anything. I paid $2500 to get into this thing. And it was pretty much pyramid scheme. You know, you'd sell travel to people and you would get a percentage of sales and then you would enroll them, you'd grow your business that way. I don't even remember what it was called, but I remember it looked so cheesy – it had a picture of a tiger or a lion on it. It was something stupid like Tiger Paw Travel. Anyway, the business went under and nobody really made any money. It was just an MLM thing that kind of came and went.

That was my first experience of failure in business, where I was just so excited to do something that I didn't even really evaluate it. I didn't go through the steps to see if it made sense. So I lost money, and I spent a lot of time trying to make it successful. And that's just a turnkey MLM business, which really doesn't require any more than good salesmanship. I guess I didn't have that either back then. I didn't have good salesmanship, and I didn't have enough diligence and smarts to evaluate if this thing was any good or not. At 18 years old, $2500 is a lot of money. That could have paid for most of my tuition at university. It was a mistake, but a lesson learned.

Later on, I got into Amway and worked my butt off while spending thousands of dollars there, when it was transitioning to Quixtar. I had 35 people in my group, I was hustling, I was going to meetings all the time, I was trying to sign people up, sell product, all that kind of stuff. And it basically got me going to conferences, big cult-like conferences, where everybody gets up there and screams "Show the plan! Show the plan – that's what it's all about. Book a meeting from a meeting." All these things they used to say. You'd see the Diamonds, the diamond level, all the rich people up on stage and like "Wow, I want to be like that." And while I failed there, I had 35 people in my group, and I'd say my biggest check ever was $150. I had poured thousands of dollars into it in education, tapes, books – they had a tape of the week program, book of the month or whatever it was. And these conferences, and the travel, plus all the time I spent and all the support materials. Man! That business makes more money off the education than anything else. But it was a good experience. I learned a lot. I finally said, "Okay, I'm done with this – 35 people and I'm generating $150. This is crazy. Forget about it. I'm doing everybody's work for them. I don't have time to waste."

"I didn't have good salesmanship, and I didn't have enough diligence and smarts to evaluate if this thing was any good or not."

Again, I didn't really do my homework. Do I want to do a MLM business? How do people respond to it? How do they perceive me? How much money can I make? What's the financial opportunity? How many people do I need to be able to have a financial return? I didn't go through that process. And again, it was an MLM business. I learned a lot of very valuable things. But where I'm going with this is: there was a bigger lesson learned about doing your diligence for a business.

The when I ended my last year university, I did a post-graduate program at the same time in college, and it was an ecommerce, entrepreneurship, and international business course all rolled into one. It was a 10-month post-grad intensive. And it was the first ever ecommerce course, or post-graduate diploma program offered in Canada. So I said, "Okay, this great, this is cool. Ecommerce is going to be big. International business of course makes sense. Entrepreneurship – hey, I love that, I'm entrepreneurial."

"I didn't really do my homework. Do I want to do a MLM business? How do people respond to it? How do they perceive me? How much money can I make? What's the financial opportunity? How many people do I need to be able to have a financial return?"

So I took it. And I met a lot of interesting people. All the profs were business owners that were successful, had a lot of insight to share. It was a really good course, but where the real value came out of was I met some people who wanted to start a business. And we started a business in 1999, which was a trust mark business. A trust mark is a seal basically that you see on a website, or packaging, or whatever it might be, that you know that this stuff is approved or safe. An example of a trust mark would be the USDA Organic seal on organic food. It would be the privacy stamp for Trustee, knowing that your privacy is safe. It would be CSA Approved. That would be a trust mark. So an independent third party that reviews the product and/or service and says, "Yes, this is safe. You can consume it, you can use it, you can share your information. Everything is fine."

We developed a trust mark for business for online business. Kind of like the Trustee privacy seal, where we would do an audit of the business, we'd evaluate their collection information, your email, your first name, all that kind of stuff, your last name, your credit card – is that secure? Will that be stored in a secure way? Is it encrypted? All that kind of stuff. And then, any transactional information, is that stored and secure? And is it a legitimate business? And what we'd do was a three-step audit process, and then we'd award that company a trust mark.

"We developed a trust mark business for online business. Kind of like the Trustee privacy seal, where we would do an audit of the business, we'd evaluate their collection information, your email, your first name, all that kind of stuff, your last name, your credit card – is that secure?"

Why did this business come to be? Well, the Boston Consulting Group's market research, in conjunction with the federal government in Canada, known as Industry Canada showed there was a need. Canada commissioned a multi-million dollar report, which basically showed that there was a need for the private sector to take over on personal information protection. The government wanted to give the guidelines, but didn't really want to enforce it per se. They really wanted the private sector to come out with solutions and innovations to protect people.

What the government ended up creating was the PIPEDA standards. PIPEDA is the *Personal Information Privacy Electronic Documents Act*, which basically said that you should be following these guidelines. But they wanted the private sector to enforce it. So we went in and followed the PIPEDA guidelines and best practices for the ecommerce and consumer electronic security. We went through it and the challenge was that we really had to educate people on our mark. The mark itself is useless unless people know who you are and that there's weight in that mark. This was a gap – we didn't think about this. We had to go to get money to advertise our mark to make sure that it instilled trust. And we went to multiple venture capitalist firms and said, "Okay, here's what we need." And a lot of them would just look at us and say, "Listen guys, you don't have any sales. You don't have a proof of concept yet. You need to prove to us that this stuff works before we fork over the money."

> *"We had to go to get money to advertise our mark to make sure that it instilled trust. And we went to multiple venture capitalist firms."*

Then they were saying, "Do you know how much money you need to market this thing?" I had a VC firm tell me $250 million. $250 million? Here I was in my last year university, just fresh out of university/college, in marketing. Sure that's great, but no practical experience in understanding how much money I actually needed to market this thing.

To me, $250 million seemed like a lot of money, but I didn't know – is that how much companies spend? Now I know today, and I would have told this guy he's out to lunch and that we can do it for much cheaper, and here's how we do it.

> *"I had a VC firm tell me $250 million. $250 million? Here I was in my last year of university, just fresh out… in marketing. No practical experience in understanding how much money I actually needed to market this thing."*

But back then, I was saying, "Oh no, we need that?" And I spent the next 24 hours building a media plan, a marketing plan that was $250 million – TV, Super Bowl ads, you name it, everything, billboards, web advertising, everything. And it really went nowhere, frankly. The business just kind of caved in onto itself.

The big part of it was my partners. My partners just didn't have integrity. They were hiding information, financial information so the books didn't make any sense. I had an accountant lined up to do pro bono work to manage our books, and they didn't want to do that. Turns out they were using the money from federal investments, which is called HRDC in Canada to use for personal gain. We had funding from Human Resources Development Canada, we had funding from government, other sources of government, through Industry Canada called FEDNOR. We had free office space from the university, free office space from the college, and we got a lot of PR from the political candidates. A lot of the politicians were really moving on trying to transition the local economy into a tech economy, so they latched on and saw it as a good PR vehicle to forward their agenda.

We were in the right place at the right time in many ways, but I had the wrong partners. We didn't do enough work in what it would take to succeed financially, what it would take to be successful in the marketplace. And frankly, I didn't do enough diligence there on my side. I just wasn't experienced enough. I made mistakes. I ended up co-signing for computers that the business couldn't pay for. My partners ended up leaving the city and the province, and so I couldn't go after them – the jurisdiction was provincial – because they owed a lot of wages to people and myself. I ended getting my wage paid for by HRDC, but we used that money for office expenses, which ended up in my partner's pockets because they just used it to pay their rent and their car, and that's why they didn't want to show the books.

> **"We were in the right place at the right time in many ways, but I had the wrong partners. We didn't do enough work in what it would take to succeed financially."**

I made a lot of mistakes there and I had a lawyer evaluate everything. And he said, "Listen Darren, you just got screwed. And you can try to go through the courts, but probably nothing will happen. I'd recommend going through Ministry of Labor to try to get that money back." It was something like $25, $30 grand. And keep in mind, I am, at this point 24 years old. Got a lot of school debt. Don't have any money. Don't have any money to pay for lawyers. Thought I was going to be rich with this.com start up. The market dried up. VCs weren't spending the money and they were saying that I needed proven sales and I needed $250 million in marketing to build a brand. I had partners that were crooks and dishonest, and hiding things. And I just said "Screw it, I'm walking away." I left the business. The business folded entirely. It was really bad. They falsified T4 slips for what I made. And it was just nasty. I wasn't the founder of the company. My partners were the founders of the company, and I came in for the sales and marketing component.

"I made a lot of mistakes… it was something like $25, $30 grand. I thought I was going to be rich with this.com start up. The market dried up. VCs weren't spending the money… I had partners that were crooks and dishonest, and hiding things."

I didn't do my homework. And I wish I knew – like many people – I wish I knew then what I know today. I would have approached that business differently. Much differently. My hope is that I can pass along some information to you so you don't make those same mistakes.

What I've done over the years is evaluated many different products, as a business, as a brand to bring to market. And I was on a team that was really about developing the pipeline. It's called the new product development pipeline. And we just ended up throwing products out like crazy: "Oh, that's cool, I think that's good, whatever." No real evaluation process. And in order to be successful and really minimize your exposure, you need to go through a screening process. And for large organizations they call that stage-gate. You don't need to follow the whole thing exactly as per stage-gate, which is a discipline through project management. But there are core elements in evaluating a business that I think are important.

What this does is bring us into the lean business concept from Eric Ries and *The Lean Startup* book, which is a phenomenal book – I highly recommend you read that. It brings in some corporate disciplines for larger Fortune 500 companies, the P&Gs of the world. And then it also brings in some practical knowhow in how to set some things up. This model that I use, which has helped me build hundreds of millions of dollars in product launches.

"I've evaluated many different products, as a business, as a brand to bring to market. There are core elements in evaluating a business that I think are important… the lean business concept. The model has helped me build hundreds of millions of dollars in product launches."

The process for starting up the business is really about identifying what your unique sustainable value proposition is. What really makes you different? And is that difference sustainable? Can somebody just copy you right away or do you have some sort of intellectual property protection there? Do you have a patent? Do you have some sort of process knowledge that nobody else has? Something unique that can't really be duplicated? Is there some sort of trade secret there that really helps you insulate against competition? Maybe you have a supplier that you have rights to, you have some sort of agreement, a licensing agreement with. Something that's sustainable is really what you're looking for here, a really good point of difference.

> *"The process for starting up the business is really about identifying what your unique sustainable value proposition is. What makes you different? And is that difference sustainable? Is that point of difference important to your target audience?"*

And then secondly, is that point of difference important to your target audience? Now that leads to the next thing: Who is your target audience? Is there a need for your product or service? I recommend developing an avatar or a persona. Maybe you're selling a vacuum, and your vacuum is extremely ergonomic and it's got a patented comfort handle that's gel-like. So people who have cramps in their hands, or arthritis, whatever, they can use this. Then maybe your target audience, your persona would be Jane. Jane is 55 years old. She has rheumatoid arthritis or osteoarthritis. She has difficulty holding a vacuum, so this product here makes it very comfortable to use, very easy to use, etc. So this gives you an idea of where to go with that.

Then your third thing would be: How big is the market? What is the opportunity at hand? So what is the financial opportunity? How many Janes are there out there? Are you going to go after this nationally? Is it

U.S.? Is it Canada? Is it international? Are you going to start up regionally? How are you going to roll this thing out? So what is the financial opportunity? What's your distribution strategy? If this thing is a service, is it digital distribution? Is it scalable? Is it just a one-on-one basis? Is it more of a consulting nature? If it's a product, what outlets are you going to go at for retail? What distributors are you going to target? Are you not going to do distributors? Are you going to do direct sales? What does that look like?

Then the other thing would be, do you have the resources to do it? Meaning, do you have the human resources and the talent? Do you have the proper sales team? Do you personally have the know-how? So you need to check those boxes off. Do you have the firepower to do it?

"How big is the market? What is the opportunity at hand? What is the financial opportunity? Do you have the resources to do it?"

Next thing to look at is, do you have the technical ability to do it? Do you or your organization have it? If you're manufacturing something, do you have the manufacturing technical capability? Do you have a manufacturing partner that has that? Or, if it's a service, do you have that know-how in order to execute it, or the software… do you have to code something that helps deliver that for you? Do you have the rights to that software, do you have to code something? Do you have the right team to do that?

Then you have to take a look at the competition. This relates to your unique sustainable value proposition. But evaluate your competition. Who are they? Where are they? How much money are they making? How is their product or service compared to yours? What is their growth like? What market are they going after? Is it your same market or not? Where are the gaps that you see that you can really exploit?

And more importantly, how will they react when you enter the market? What is their reaction going to be?

"Look at the competition. How much money are they making? What market are they going after? What gaps can you exploit? How will they react when you enter the market?

For the vacuum example, maybe a competitor would be the iRobot vacuum. Maybe in their advertising, they've never targeted somebody with arthritis, but now all they have to do is put that in their advertising, say "Great for people with arthritis." How are you going to react to that? So you need to plan those things out. Will they discount their product or service to try to squeeze you out of the marketplace? Will they do comparative advertising against your product or service? Will they try to go after your distribution to squeeze you out and get exclusivity? Will they come after you from a legal perspective if they potentially think you're infringing on intellectual property rights? All these questions you have to ask yourself.

Then one of the last, most important things is regulatory and legal constraints. Is there a challenge from a regulatory perspective? Do you have to apply for certain safety precautions? Is there a CSA approval? Do you have to have an FDA approval on this? Is there any sort of manufacturing qualifications or a partner that you have to select in order to qualify for selling your product in the market? Regulatory constraints, and any legal constraints are real barriers that can cripple a business. You need to understand this.

"Is there a challenge from a regulatory perspective? Is there any sort of manufacturing qualifications or a partner that you have to select in order to qualify for selling your product in the market?"

The very last thing is just financial projections. How much money are you going to make? How much money are you going to make in year 1, year 2, year 3? What's your exit strategy? Are you going to want to bring this company public? Is this thing going to be a small organization? Is it just you, a one-man operation? Is it going to be just a small business, less than 50 people? Medium-sized? How much money do you need to get this thing started? Where's that capital coming from? Are you going to do a bank loan? Do you have your own startup capital? Are you going to do a Kickstarter or Indiegogo crowdfunding campaign? Do you want to go after private equity? Do you want to leverage a private equity partner's resources? Are they going to run it? What percentage of shares do you want? I'm giving you a lot of questions, but these are things that you really have to ask yourself when you look at the financials.

> **"How much money are you going to make in year 1, year 2, year 3? What's your exit strategy? How much money do you need to get this thing going?**

Ultimately, what you really want to do is to build that projection. Any capital costs… Do you have to rent office space, phone systems, any manufacturing equipment? Do you have to buy any inventory? Do you have to hold inventory? Do you have any licensing fees that you have to pay for? Do you have a call center you have to pay for? Leasehold improvements in office space? Do you have professional dues that are required? There's so many things, you can go down the list. Sales and marketing expenses? In year 1, are you profitable? What's your cash burn rate? So how many weeks and months is it going to take to be cash positive based on your projections? Are you going to go after retail, if you have a product? Do you have a sales team to do it, or are you going to outsource that to a brokerage? What percentage of sales are you going to give them? How is it going to impact your profitability? All of these things will need to be mapped out with a profit and loss statement.

It's really important to go through these screening processes. Then a big part of the analysis is the viability of the product as it relates to the financial implications and market acceptance. You don't want to go and spend a lot of money on focus groups and quantitative research. You can spend $30,000 easily on that. This is where the lean startup model comes into play. This is where direct response marketers and Internet marketers shine.

"Go through these screening processes. A big part of the analysis is the viability of the product as it relates to the financial implications and market acceptance."

I would recommend going through the model I just explained. And it doesn't have to be perfect, but just put what you know in there today. Just high-level, the best you can do. However, now what you want to do is you want to test your product or service. Now you need to do a minimal viable product, put up a website, a landing page – you can use LeadPages.net or Unbounce.com. All you need is Optimize Press if you're a WordPress guy. You need to have some visuals, so get a designer. Go on Fiverr.com or 99 Designs, whatever you want to use, to draft something up, a mockup of what your product or service is. Then get an email marketing system, like a MailChimp, Aweber, Get Response, Exact Target, there's a whole bunch of them. Then get a domain name. So let's use the vacuum example. Let's call this vacuum EZ Vac, for lack of a better name. EZ Vac. Get ezvac.com if it's available. You want to map that domain – use GoDaddy. GoDaddy's great. I use them for a lot of my domain names. They're pretty cheap, they've got great service, never any issues with them. There's a lot of domain providers out there.

You can use who you prefer, but that's who I use. You want to map that domain to Unbounce or LeadPages.

> *"Test your product or service… do a minimal viable product, put up a website, a landing page… an email marketing system… get a domain name."*

Then what you want to do is have your designer do a 3D rendering prototype of your vacuum and the packaging, buy some stock images, write some sales copy, set a price for it. So let's just say, set a price of $300. And you haven't even produced anything yet. That's okay. What you want to do is have that mockup, have that offer at $300, have your sales copy. If you can do a mock video, great, even better for a sales pitch if you have that ability. Again you can use Fiver or 99 Designs to do these things. And then do ads. Do some Facebook targeted ads, targeting people with arthritis, in that age demographic, in that geographic region you want. Direct them to that landing page. On that landing page you have your product, your offer, what the problem is – "Hey, are your hands too sore? You have arthritis and you can't vacuum? Well, we've got the solution for you: it's EZ Vac. Safe, fast, effective, comfortable technology where you can get back to having a clean house again."

> *"Have your designer do a 3D rendering prototype… write some sales copy, set a price for it. And you haven't even produced anything yet."*

Then you have your offer on there and you have an email linked up to the web form, where it's like "Okay, enter to buy now." And you buy now, and you have an email auto-responder saying, "Okay, thank you very much for your offer. Shipping will happen in 8-12 weeks. This is a pre-sales offer. And we'll be in touch with next steps."

Basically, you run that. A hundred orders is what you need for statistical significance to determine if it's a really viable product. You'll know what your conversion rates are, how responsive your target audience is to your product. Then once you have that money in hand, you have 2 decisions. You can say, "Well, that wasn't effective enough to pursue. I was off-base. Let me modify that. How about I try a different target audience? How about I try different messaging? Maybe I'll try a different price point." And this is where you can get into different A/B splits. So that landing page is option A. Then you go to option B. You modify maybe your headline, maybe you modify the potential design of your product, if you have that flexibility. You modify your target audience – maybe you say you want to go after house moms who don't have arthritis issues. Maybe it's just that they want a comfortable vacuum for once. And then what you'll find is, you want to just only change one variable in these A/B splits, not too many variables because you want to isolate what the difference is. And by doing that, you'll find out what the right message is, what the right audience is, what the right price point is, and what the right creative is. And from there, you can then extrapolate what your real financial opportunity is, who your target market is.

"100 orders is what you need for statistical significance to determine if it's a really viable product. You'll know your conversion rates and how responsive your target audience is to your product."

This is the way to do quick and dirty and lean market research that is the most important. Why? People will vote with their wallet! This is what it's all about. Save your money on the focus groups. Save your money for that stuff. Go with the lean startup model. And by doing this, you'll have pre-sales information. You'll have money in your account. By the way, you'll have to hook up a PayPal account of course or a

Stripe account. Imagine selling your product or service before it exists… Money in your account to actually buy inventory, to spend money on building this up. Or you can actually just say, "Okay, we're going to re-fund your money, customer. The business is not going through. Thank you very much for your patronage." But at least you have their email. And if you have their email, you can go and remarket your next idea to them. You see what I mean? That's the beauty of it. That's the beauty of the process here.

> *"People vote with their wallet! Imagine selling your product or service before it exists… money in your account to actually buy inventory, to spend money on building this up."*

What you can do is get that domain name. You can register your business if you want to – you don't necessarily have to. You can get those LeadPages or Unbounce landing pages developed by yourself; you don't even need a graphic designer to do that. It's super-simple drag and drop, templates of what works. You can use Fiver or 99 Designs to develop some mockups, visual mockups, 3D renderings of your product and your logo. And you run the test. And you get pre-sales information. From that, if you want more money – depending on what your startup costs are – you take that pre-sales information and then you go and develop a Kickstarter or Indiegogo campaign. You say, "Okay, here's my product. Here's the target market." You do a video series, videos explaining what it is and saying in pre-sales, you sold a lot. It's very effective. And then you do pre-sales on your Kickstarter campaign, or your crowdfunding campaign. And then from there, you set your targets, and if you don't hit your targets, you don't get your money, but you've already done these pre-sales, you've already tested your product or service out. You know what the expected outcome would be. You know what messaging works, you know what visuals work, what creative works. You're bringing that over to your Kickstarter campaign, and you have a very good chance for success. Where you could then not have to give up equity to your business. That's very powerful.

If you want that help and you want that leadership, then maybe you do want to go the equity route. And if you're looking for private equity, then there are a lot of firms out there. Angel.co is a good example of a site that you can visit to find some information on what startups are getting money, who's investing in them. There's a few other angel investor websites out there. There are services that can help you with consulting, like score.org, which is a service of all retired business executives that will help and advise you on your business. There's a lot of different things out there for you, but like I said, if you don't have to give up the equity, if you don't want to, there's options there for you. Those services and that process will really help you build your business.

> *"Angel.co is a good example of a site that you can visit to find some information on what startups are getting money, who's investing in them. There are services that can help you with consulting, like score.org."*

Again, it's kind of bringing a couple concepts together: the lean startup model and the stage-gate process. So if you can bring those disciplines together, infuse them together, you have a really powerful formula for evaluating a business concept, and planning it out and being mindful of how to scale and succeed. And I wish I had these tools when I was younger. Because before we invested all this time and money in building up this trust mark, and having 11 people on staff, and all these meetings and money and office space and computers, I would have just slapped up a seal on a website and see if it affected conversion rates on their website. Frankly, that's all I would have done. "Hey, can we do a test? Here's it for free. We just want to see if it impacts your conversion rates." If it does, great, I got a case study here. I know I have proof of concept. Awesome, here we go. That's what I would have done. It would have saved a lot of heartache because nobody wanted to buy and spend the money. I would have tested out price points too. Then I would have made sure I've done all the research. Who are my competitors? What are they doing? What are people willing to pay? What are my financial projects? Anyways, mistakes are only lessons. We get wiser; we become a little more intelligent in how we approach things.

> *"I wish I had these tools when I was younger. I would have just slapped up a seal on a website and see if it affected conversion rates on their website. If it does... I know I have a proof of concept."*

So I hope there's some lessons in here for you on how to build your business, how to start it and evaluate it, and not be out of pocket so much, and to be mindful of future success. And then also, know when you have a winner and know when you have a loser before you invest a lot of time and money in something.

Hopefully you start your next business or business unit very soon, and you follow a similar process and have a lot of success with it. I wish you the best of luck. There's a lot of opportunity out there for you. Every single day, people are becoming more and more successful with new brands, new products, new services. There are a lot of exciting things happening out there, and you definitely should have your share.

Chapter 2

You vs. You

Do you have the imposter syndrome? Where it's a you vs. you mentality? If you know what I'm talking about, intuitively, you've probably been there yourself or are going through it right now.

> *"Do you have the imposter syndrome? Where it's a you vs. you mentality? You've probably been there yourself."*

It all started for me at a very young age. I think was 13 when I got my first job. And it was a really rough job actually. It was at a greenhouse and a nursery, not too far from where I grew up, about a 15-minute bike ride in the country, up in Northern Canada. It was an after-school and summer job. Like I said, I was 13 years old, didn't have a social insurance number, so I probably shouldn't even have been working. There was this building called the soil shed. And exactly like it sounds, it was full of dirt. My job was to shovel dirt all day, mix it up with some fertilizer, some peat moss, nitrogen, bag it, put it on a forklift and move it out to the yard for it to be sold for potting soil. I also had to get shipments of evergreen trees around Christmas, or they would get some apple trees, or whatever it might be. We'd take them into the soil shed, prune the roots, put them in a pot, dig up our soil, put it in there, water it, shrink-wrap it, and then put them out on the yard for sale.

> *"I was 13 when I got my first job… My job was to shovel dirt all day, mix it up with some fertilizer, some peat moss, nitrogen, bag it, put it on a forklift, and move it out to the yard for it to be sold for potting soil."*

So, imagine you're 13 years old and working in a building full of dirt all day, shoveling it, using it with your hands, pruning trees. It was unbelievable. And I worked for some great people. It was a really hardworking experience. You'd go home and blow your nose and dirt would come out. You had dirt in your ears. It was just disgusting. Your throat would be raw because you're breathing in dirt. It really was insanitary.

And I remember in the summer too, they would give me odd jobs, so I'd go in the greenhouse. You know how hot a greenhouse is on a sunny day – over 100 degrees. I'd go underneath all the tables where all the flowers are, on my hands and knees and weed all of the weeds that had come up in the soil. So a greenhouse is probably about 200 feet long and maybe about 25 feet wide. I'd have to go down each one of the rows. And they had about 25 of these big long greenhouses that I had to go through and weed.

The greenhouse and nursery, by the way, was called Vanderwees Greenhouse and Nursery up in Thunder Bay, Ontario. And if you're from Thunder Bay or Northern Ontario, you know what I'm talking about. If you ever go there, I'd recommend that you visit Vanderwees and take a look around. It's a great spot.

But my point is that I always looked at the owners; it was a family-run business. The owners had so much passion, so much energy. And they worked hard, but they had a very nice lifestyle. They were living close by to the business. They would get workers to work on their yard, to landscape and everything. They built great relationships with customers. You could see what they were doing. They were a very customer-centric organization and they really led by example. And I remember thinking "Wow, that's what I want to do. I want to be like that. I want to be the boss. Not just the boss. I want to be the one with a stake in it – a business run by my culture, run the way I want it to be run." That was at a very young age. And I thought, "Well, I'm willing to work hard. I can probably do that."

> *"The owners had so much passion, so much energy... They built great relationships with customers. They were a very customer-centric organization and they really led by example. And I remember thinking 'Wow, that's what I want to do'."*

But I had no idea how to go about it. At 13 years old, the Internet really wasn't around yet. It was a different economy. This is in the late '80s, almost '90. So I really had no idea. And then the next year I heard the word *entrepreneur*. I don't know where it was; I don't remember truly. I think it was my cousin through marriage who mentioned the word *entrepreneur*. I think he worked two weeks his entire life for somebody else. He ran a construction business; he was a contractor in the Detroit area, very successful and my mentor over the years. He had an energy about him; he had this passion, this enthusiasm, and this great lifestyle in Grosse Pointe, Michigan, which if you know that area is one of the wealthiest areas in North America, just outside of Detroit. I was just like "Man, I want to be like that when I grow up." He was just a phenomenal human being. Not only did I admire him for what he accomplished, I really loved him as a human being.

> *"At 13 years old... I heard the word entrepreneur."*

So when I heard the word *entrepreneur*, I was like "Wow, it's so seductive. That's what I want to be." And then as time went on, I continued to work and work at part-time jobs. I always worked hard. I was very competitive, still am. Always wanted to be the best, shovel the most dirt. Time myself to do things better. And then I really started working on self-development – how-to books, a really strong drive, I got heavily involved in sports. You know, I had a strong drive to really succeed. And I think that's what you need. You need that to be an entrepreneur.

When I was in grade 9, I tried out for the junior boys' basketball team. And I was tall. I was 6'1, 165 lbs in grade 9. People thought I was a senior. I was like "Man, I play basketball every single day. I can grab the rim." I thought, "I'm for sure going to make the team." I had a horrible tryout. I remember one time I was on breakaway, went for a layup, and hit the bottom of the rim. It was embarrassing. I think back and think of course I wouldn't have been picked. And that's what happened – I didn't get picked and it totally crushed me. It *crushed* me. So what I did is I practiced every single day and every night. I played during the lunch hour at my school in the gym. I played after school when I got home. Even in the wintertime, which is like -35, -40 Celsius in Thunder Bay, Ontario, I'd put my snowsuit on, put my gloves on, and I would shoot hoops with a frozen ball for a couple hours. Every night. Because I was determined to come back and make the team. Just brute force and consistent effort. Maybe I wasn't the best player, but I thought "Damn it, I'm gonna just give it my all because this is what I love. There's no other option for me. I love the game. I want to play."

> *"I didn't make my grade 9 basketball team and it crushed me. So what I did is I practiced every single day and every night... Even in wintertime... I was determined to come back and make the team. Just brute force and consistent effort."*

So every day I played, hours and hours and hours. If you know the Malcolm Gladwell's 10,000 hours rule in the book *Outliers*, you know what I'm talking about. So, the next year, the tryouts came and the coach said to me "Wow, have you been practicing?" I said, "Oh yeah, a little." I actually got picked. Not only did I get picked, I started. I played every single game. I was on the All-Star team. And over the years, I just continued to get better. One of the top players in the city, All-Star, high scoring, all that kind of stuff. It was a great experience and it was just because I worked hard at it. I never gave up and I persevered.

"The next year… Not only did I get picked, I started. I played every single game. I was on the All-Star team… A great experience and it was just because I worked hard at it. I never gave up and I persevered."

And I think it's that mentality that you need in business. You need to know when to pivot, of course, and what to focus on, but it's that perseverance, that resiliency; that's a characteristic of an entrepreneur and even a great marketer. You have to be resilient and know that it takes some time. And you also need to know what to look for, to understand when to pivot, and when to push forward. You always need to move ahead. You just can't give up. You have to go at different angles. You have to go towards the same goal. There's multiple ways to get there, but never give up. You're not a quitter. If you're a quitter, you wouldn't be reading this.

"It's that mentality you need in business. You need to know when to pivot, of course, and what to focus on, but it's that perseverance, that resiliency; that's the characteristic of an entrepreneur and even a great marketer."

So, that's my story about the personality and psychology of pushing on and resiliency. But back to entrepreneurship. When I was in my senior years of high school, I got involved in my first business. My first business was multi-level marketing. It was a travel business where you'd have to sell travel packages. And I forget the name of it, something like Tiger Tribe Travel, I just really can't remember. My girlfriend's mother worked for them and she saw something in me, that entrepreneurial edge, that marketing mindset, and she actually recruited me as an 18-year-old.

And I just embraced it. I did presentations, and I analyzed the business, and thought I was going to get rich and this is going to be amazing. I worked and worked at it and I realized people don't want to buy travel from an 18-year-old kid. I have no credibility; they don't want to believe in me. So what did I do? I quit. But, what I truly did is I pivoted – I realized that this isn't for me, so I moved on to something else.

I actually moved on to Amway, which was known at that time as Quixstar. Quixstar was their online version of Amway. This was in the late '90s, I believe. They were launching it and I was on the ground floor so I said, "Okay, I see the opportunity, I'm in." I got in there and really embraced it. I had some digital experience. I was building my own websites through html in my bedroom. My then-$3,500 computer that was a Pentium 133 – I mean it was 2 gigs of RAM – I thought that thing was a beast. Dial-up Internet… it was brutal. But I thought, "Okay, this is the next wave. This is where it's going. I'm going to get in. I'm going to get on the money train. I'm going to get ahead of the curve." Arriving at opportunity when everybody's there isn't opportunity. You want to get ahead of the curve.

> *"Arriving at opportunity when everybody's there isn't opportunity. You want to get ahead of the curve."*

So, I actually ended up building a network of 35 people, cold-calling people, following the plan. The process was called STP: show the plan. They said "How many no's does it take to get a yes?" And I'll tell you something. I went to conferences. I met the top people in the organization and they sat down one-on-one with me and said, "You can do this." I had leadership all over me and they really thought I could do it. And I believed I could do it. But what I found was I did everybody's work for them. I had a lot of people with a welfare mentality. They said, "Yeah okay, I see Darren, he's gonna work hard, seems like a bright kid. I'll hop aboard his success train and ride the coattails." And frankly, I wasn't that successful. I persevered, I worked hard, I thought I was pretty bright. But I was only making $150 a month and I was spending probably $500 a month in books and tapes and going to education seminars and buying products. I just wasn't seeing this work. So eventually what I did is I decided that okay, I think I'm just going to do my own business. I left and ended up getting involved in more multi-level marketing. I got involved in a money pyramid and believe it or not – I was 19 years old, maybe 20 years old that time – I was on phone calls with people around the world and helping them make money through a money pyramid.

I went into a travel MLM at 18 and failed, then Amway for several years and failed, then other MLM's and even cash gifting… I had cash envelopes arriving at my home, but what I learned was more valuable than even getting my college degrees.

It's crazy. I was actually getting cash in the mail in an envelope folded in a magazine. It was all above board. It would say, "This is a gift." You can give up to $10,000 to an individual per year. You have to have the documentation, knowing that you will not expect anything back. There's a way to do it properly. I got involved in that and in a year, I can't remember how many thousands of dollars I made. And I was getting cash in envelopes! It was mind blowing. I eventually got out of that, though.

I got into a multi-level marketing program that educated people on how to retire quickly, and how to set up their finances. Kind of like the Dave Ramsey approach. So I did that for a while. Then I got involved in organic household cleaning products, called Pure Essence if I recall. It was biodegradable, all that kind of stuff. Because I was passionate about that, I'm a very health-oriented guy and didn't want perfumes and chemicals so I did that. Didn't go. So I quit. I pivoted.

Then I got involved in a certified organic skin care line of products out of Australia, called One Group. I got a little bit of traction on it, and I decided no, I'm going to pivot again. In 2002 I started blogging – a business blog and marketing blog, with my name Darren Contardo and called it The Netrepreneur. I did that for years, off and on – didn't really get a lot of traffic, got some positive comments, but it was more of a hobby. I didn't know how I was going to monetize it. I was just kind of spitting ideas out and my talking about my business experiences.

Then I went on to register a domain called ILoveOrganics.com and built an organics community because I'm really passionate about organic living and eating healthy. And that actually, believe it or not, is still going on. It requires some effort and some work to really foster community and I realized that while this is going on, I'm really passionate about some other things. So I got involved in some other businesses. This is where I've arrived today. I keep on pivoting. I started a business with my wife, really helping her with HIT Club Fitness. We set up her own gym in our house. She is a personal trainer in CrossFit, CanFitPro, other certifications. She is a fitness author and wrote a book. And we've built a business for her so she actually could quit her job and do that from home and raise our kids. And that's exactly what we've done. We built a business that she can live off of, which is excellent.

But during this time I realized what I really want to do; I really want to help people, and I really want to help them with health and fitness and feeling good about themselves, but also want to help them with finances, I want to help them with the human psychology of being successful. I want to help them with their businesses, with marketing, and help them truly reach success. To fast-track through all the crap, all the stuff that doesn't work, and help guide them to something that will reap rewards. So that's one of the reasons why The Marketer's Commute has been born. Because I have an entrepreneur's heart.

> *"I realized what I really want to do; I really want to help people with health and fitness, feeling good about themselves, but also want to help them with finances, and the human psychology of being successful."*

I gave you a bit of my journey. And there are other components too, but the largest struggle has just been the psychology of it all. Like, can I actually do it? Is something wrong with me? Am I good enough? Am I smart enough? Remember Stuart Smalley on SNL? "I'm good enough. I'm smart enough. And doggone it, people like me."

> *"The largest struggle has just been the psychology of it all. Like, can I actually do it? Is something wrong with me? Am I good enough? Am I smart enough? Remember Stuart Smalley on SNL?"*

I think everybody goes through that. Am I smart enough to do this? Am I good enough? Do I have enough credibility? Do I believe in myself? What if I fail? Will I fail? And I think there are a lot of sayings out there, a lot of motivational quotes, but I think you have to understand something. You have to really say, "Do I have the persistence? Do I believe in it?" And the answer is "Absolutely. Absolutely, you believe in it." You wouldn't be starting something, reading this book, and taking a proactive approach to your life if you didn't.

I believe you can do it. There are a lot of people that you influence and you probably don't even know it. But that's psychology, you know. Am I good enough? Am I smart enough? Are there going to be naysayers out there? Are people going to pick me apart? Am I going to crumble from it? No. You know what? Be confident. Take risks. Take calculated risks. But take them. Believe in yourself and push forward. Confidence is contagious. People feel it. They get it. If you're not confident and believe in yourself, people won't follow you. And you'll make mistakes, you absolutely will. But you can't let yourself get in the way. It's you vs. you.

"I believe you can do it. There are a lot of people that you influence and you probably don't even know it."

You have to understand why it is you're doing what you're doing. Why? Is the "why" worth it? Whether you're working for somebody else as a marketer or building your own small business or entrepreneur or online marketer. You have to ask yourself "Is the 'why' worth it?" Maybe you want to be at home with your kids and build a lifestyle where you can work from anywhere you want, you can live anywhere you want. And if that's your why, it's absolutely worth it.

And what if you fail? What if you go out there and you work the system and you do what I've outlined in the book, and what other experts have told you to do, and it doesn't work for you? What then? I'll tell you what. Just get up and you pivot a little bit. You try something else. You still move forward. Because nobody is going to give it to you. You have to get it yourself. And people, they'll help you, but you have to want it.

"And what if you fail? Just get up and you pivot a little bit. You try something else. You still move forward. Because nobody is going to give it to you. You have to get it yourself."

Don't get in the way of yourself. I've been doing it my whole life. There's a little voice in the back of your head, your subconscious – it's like the elephant and the ant syndrome. You have that ant that is your conscious mind, and the elephant which is your subconscious mind. That elephant will just roam about, and it will just bring that ant wherever unless you train your mind, you train that ant to lead that elephant. You train your conscious mind to lead that subconscious elephant. And if you can do that, you're the master of your own domain.

It's okay to be vulnerable. There's a ton of strength in being vulnerable. And in being a marketer, being an entrepreneur, small business owner, where nothing is guaranteed and everything you do is based on results. And that's the measure of success. That's difficult. But, you'll never get to success unless you're okay being vulnerable. Think about the moments in life that are the most rewarding for you. A pivotal time in your relationship, perhaps with your significant other, where you laid it out on the line, you became very vulnerable. How did that work out for you? Perhaps you got married. Maybe you had kids. Or maybe, you had to pivot. But you needed to be vulnerable and express how you felt to be able to move forward in the direction that you needed to. The same goes with business. The same goes with marketing. You have to be willing to put yourself out there, and face fear, and be judged.

> *"You'll never get to success unless you're okay with being vulnerable. Think about the moments in life that are the most rewarding for you. A pivotal time in your relationship, perhaps with your significant other, where you laid it out on the line, you became very vulnerable. How did that work out for you?"*

But the people who try to put chinks in your armor, dents in your armor, they're the ones that are the most insecure. They're the peanut gallery that's just willing and waiting to judge anybody, but what have they done? They're too scared to take action. They're too scared to fail. They're too scared to succeed.

> *"People who try to put chinks in your armor, dents in your armor, they're the ones that are the most insecure… They're too scared to take action. They're too scared to fail. They're too scared to succeed."*

I guarantee you if you talk to people who have been successful, who have made themselves vulnerable and persevered and were resilient and pivoted when necessary, they won't judge you. They'll be there to support you. So being an entrepreneur and being a marketer – a successful one – requires you to face fear, requires you to be vulnerable.

And that's been a big journey for me. Quite honestly, I've talked to a professional. I was in therapy for four years, really dealing with this. And I realized that it never really was the businesses; it was always me. I probably got to that level of, "Oh, it's going to break through," and it scared me. And I held myself back. I was always gung-ho, getting into this, getting into that, talked a big game, did some stuff, started a lot of stuff, didn't finish it, because it started to get real. I'm like, "Oh no, people are starting to depend on me. Wait a minute, can I do this?" And I struggled. I'm telling you, struggling for 20 years from the entrepreneurship angle, it's difficult. From the marketing angle, when it's other people's money and businesses, I was really a lot more willing to take the risks and test things out because it wasn't my name as much. It wasn't my business on the line. Sure it was my reputation and my career, but it's a little bit different. You can hide behind it. You can hide behind the corporate fail. When it's you, when it's your brand, your business, your personal brand, it's really difficult. It's a different world. You're very vulnerable. So it's okay. You're not alone. Everybody goes through this. But you need to be willing to accept some vulnerability. It will be absolutely worth it.

"I held myself back. I was always gung-ho, getting into this, getting into that, talked a big game, did some stuff, started a lot of stuff, didn't finish it, because it started to get real… From the marketing angle I was really a lot more willing to take the risks and test things out because it wasn't my name as much."

So I just finally said "Okay, I'm going to go after it. I'm going to do multiple businesses in health, fitness, and marketing, including a podcast and this book." This is absolutely a fit. This is the right thing to do. And it took a lot of years of experience, a culmination of events and people and failures and pivoting, and psychological battles with myself to get here today.

I never had a problem building another business for other people, consulting, building hundreds of millions of dollars in new brands and sales for other companies, but when it came to me, it was a different story. And it was just me in the way. So don't let yourself get in the way.

"Don't let yourself get in the way… Surround yourself with positive people, people who have the same abundance mindset, not the scarcity mindset."

Surround yourself with positive people, people who have the same abundance mindset, not the scarcity mindset. Challenge yourself to be vulnerable, not only in your career, in your business, but in life, with your relationships. It will absolutely work in your favor. It has in mine. Otherwise I wouldn't be here today talking to you and trying to help you build a great brand. You can do it. And it's a heck of a lot of fun.

Chapter 3

Leadership

This is a marketing book, but leadership is critical as a marketing leader, as a senior executive, a manager, or as owner of your own business. You're managing your customers, plus you have to show some leadership in the marketplace. I'm not the be-all end-all expert at leadership; I only can draw upon my experiences and what I've read and what I've seen. And it's a very interesting topic because leadership is one of those things that makes such a significant impact to your business.

You can choose to be a leader in your business with your staff, people on your team, or not. And here's the difference. Leadership is one of those things where if it's really good, you notice it. And if it's really bad, you notice it.

> *"Leadership is one of those things where if it's really good, you notice it. And if it's really bad, you notice it."*

So what are the core elements of leadership, just from a human perspective? Let's not even talk about your brand, your product, your service, your company – just you managing people. What are the core elements of leadership? Well, I think the first thing is a leader sets an example.

The biggest question I always ask myself is: What would I do when nobody's looking? And I think that comes down to integrity. So what would *you* do when nobody's looking? Do you change when the spotlight's on you? Do you say something in front of your leadership to position yourself as an authority or a know-it-all or that you're in control? And then when the truth comes out, when the door closes and they're gone and you're sitting there by yourself, do you say "What the hell's going on? I don't know. I have to go to my staff and ask them all these questions and see if they can help me." Or do you go and turn around and lambaste them? You know, if something goes wrong, do you throw your team under the bus, or blame somebody else? Or do you take responsibility and say, "I'm the leader. That's what I need to do. It falls with me. Let me figure it out."

> *"What do you do when nobody is looking? Do you change when the spotlight is on you? Do you act like you're in control but really wonder what the hell is going on?"*

So those are core elements of leadership. I think it comes down to integrity. How much integrity do you have? Because integrity is not a tangible thing, but it's so critically important. And the test that I give myself is: When I put my head down at the end of the day on my pillow, if I fall asleep quickly, that means I've operated with integrity because I have a clean conscience. And if I don't, that means I'm not operating with integrity and I don't have a clean conscience. Now I will say that I fall asleep within 5 seconds usually, so I always tend to operate my day, my practices, with the utmost integrity. But your staff, your teams, your management, your customers, they all see that. Your family – they see that integrity. And it becomes palpable. It becomes something that's part of your character. So the integrity and what happens when nobody's looking is of the utmost importance.

The second thing is: Do you actually do what you say? Do you? When you say or think, "I'm going to go do this." Do you follow up? Make sure it's done? See it to the end? That's another important aspect to leadership. If you say "Yeah, I'll take care of that, whatever," and you don't, that's a definite blemish on your leadership potential. People will begin not to take you for your word. And your word is everything. If you say you're going to do something, do something! Because eventually people won't believe in you.

> **"Do what you say you're going to do. Otherwise you blemish your leadership potential and eventually people won't believe you."**

Now, there's another element of leadership that is critically important. And that's consistency. Are you consistent? Just like a brand, like brand equity – are you consistent in your actions, your behavior? Here's a funny thing about people: people seek order. The way you organize your files, the way you organize your day, the way you organize your finances. That's why people are usually resistant to change. So if you think you're a leader and you zigzag a lot, and you're indecisive, and you're not consistent – one day you're in a great mood, one day you're not – that is so unsettling for your employees, team members, and even customers. People won't follow you because there's no predictability. They don't know what they're getting into. You don't want to be that guy, or that woman. You want to be consistent. Just like a brand – consistent messaging, consistent experience. Just like a McDonald's, you walk in anywhere in the world, it's going to be consistent. If it's different all the time, you don't know what you're going to get yourself into. You don't trust that you're going to have a good experience. Your team wants to trust you. Prove to them that they can.

"Are you consistent? People seek order and are resistant to change. So if you think you're a leader and you zigzag a lot, and you're indecisive, and you're not consistent it's unsettling for employees, team members, and even customers."

Another core element of leadership that I've seen through my life is action. I know I said earlier, "Do what you say" but action, consistent action is absolutely critical. You gotta have some wins, you gotta show proof, proof of concept that shows, "Yeah, I'm working hard towards this." Because everybody is looking at you as a leader, everybody. Actions speak louder than words. You have to show. Show the team, your employees, your customers, that you indeed are a leader. You can be the quietest person there, that doesn't matter.

"You can be the quietest person, that doesn't matter. Actions speak louder than words... and people follow people who act."

Another key element of leadership is influence. Do you have influence? Now this is critically important. In John C. Maxwell's book *The 21 Irrefutable Laws of Leadership*, there's a workbook called *Developing the Leader Within* that goes along with it. He talks about what leadership truly is: influence. You don't need to be the manager, the owner, the director to have influence. You can be a leader without the title, as long as you have influence. And how do you have influence? Well, you're consistent, you have consistent action, you do what you say. When the door's closed and nobody's looking, you do the right thing. You stand up for your customers and your team. You pass the praise and you take the fall. That's what great leaders do. That's why people rally behind great leaders. And a great leader can entirely transform a business. A bad leader can utterly destroy an organization, whether that's a small business or a large business.

"People rally behind great leaders – they can transform a business. On the flip side a bad leader can utterly destroy an organization, whether that's a small business or large business!"

Think about baseball. The coach, it's his responsibility if the team wins. That's what he's getting paid to do. He's getting paid to manage the talent, motivate the talent, put them in the proper position, and win ball games. Now, if the coach showed up and said, "Okay, we gotta play ball, right? Okay, okay. Umm, how many people do we need on the field? Okay, we'll just uh, alright just go out there guys, let's go win." "Okay, well what position do I play?" "Well, just go figure it out, just get it done." "Okay, well what's our strategy?" "Umm, I don't know – just win. We gotta win. Just play hard." So, the chances of you winning are low. And then the coach gets frustrated: "How come you guys aren't winning? What the hell is going on? You guys are incompetent." Really? Really? Is that the case? No, the coach's job is to go and understand the competition, understand the talent that he has in the ball club, put them in the right position, help them focus on their strengths, give them clear expectations of what's required and when it's required, and what success looks like. And when there are failures, encourage them to be better, not destroy their confidence. Because confidence is key.

I like to use the "I think" strategy. So my experience has been that people will be and perform as well as you think they can. I've had people report to me, and they've had some struggles. I brought them in behind closed doors and we talk about professional development and sometimes even personal. And I say "Listen, I see that you're struggling. I see that you're down on yourself, but let me tell you something. I believe in you. I think that you're capable of excellence. I think that you're going to be a star. I think that if you could put your mind to it, you could be a leader and make a mark in the business. I think that you have unlimited potential." And when you do that, and really mean it, you elevate the level of play. Elevate the engagement. You pump them up, you inflate them. You actually have a pump and it's like a balloon and you're inflating them full of hope, desire, confidence, energy, motivation, and inspiration. But more importantly, you're saying "You're worthy and I trust you." That comes back to you in so many ways.

> *"I use the 'I think' strategy. I tell people that I see them struggling, but let them know that I think they can do great things and realize their potential. I tell them that I believe in them, trust them, and am routing for them. It's like inflating them with hope, desire, confidence, energy, motivation, and inspiration."*

So, there's core elements there. We talked about integrity, action, confidence, inspiring people, knowing people's strengths, building good teams, being very clear on what's required, when it's required. Criticize in private, praise in public. There's all those core elements of leadership. And taking a fall for the team. That's critical because the buck stops with you as a leader. If you want to be a leader, that's what leaders do. Leaders make themselves vulnerable. And vulnerability is the greatest strength of all. If you're willing to say "Yes, I made a mistake, but I'm not going to do it again and here's why. And I'm going to work with the team. I believe in the team. Here's what we need to do to win." That's phenomenal.

> *"Leaders make themselves vulnerable. And vulnerability is the greatest strength of all."*

And now here's the interesting thing. You can bring those same elements... You the leader, individually, and you the leader in the marketplace. So think about what we said: integrity, consistency, action, all those elements. As a brand leader, as a small business leader in your community, people still look at you the same way. You have to think of it as a human being, a living entity. Are you consistent in your messaging? Are you transparent in your operations? Are you doing things with the utmost integrity as a business and as a brand? Are you treating your customers with integrity? Are you responding to them quickly? Are you trying to give them a great experience? Do you have a great return policy? Those little things. Do you position yourself as a leader? "Yes, we are the best at what we do. We are the #1 niche product. We're absolutely going to live and breathe this." Just like you do as a leader.

So that's how you do it. My approach has always been: If you're not going to be #1 at it, don't do it. If you're not going to be the absolute best, the absolute best business, brand, best you can be, don't do it. It's not worth it. Life's too short. Now if you want to just be a bottom feeder, a #2, and take what you can get, that's fine. If you just chase the dollar, it becomes very transparent. People don't follow that. Once they get wind of that, they're done. They want to know that you aspire as a business and as a brand, as something great. And that you're passionate about it. That's what market leadership is, just like human. The elements are the same.

> *"If you're not going to be #1 at it, don't do it. If you're not going to be the absolute best, the absolute best business, brand, best you can be, don't do it. It's not worth it. Life is too short."*

Leadership is an interesting topic. We can go on and on and on about it. But I want you to think about some of those elements of leadership. You, the leader, the individual, and what's required. And you, the master of your business or your brand, how to position yourself as a leader, and what actions and what integrity and what consistency and what clear communication is required. It's all on you. It's such a great responsibility. But it's such a simple thing. It truly is. That's the magical thing about it. It's all on you. You can absolutely make it, if you haven't already. And if you have, think a little bit about your leadership style and even from your marketplace and your brand perspective, your organization's perspective, how you are a leader.

Chapter 4

Small Is the New Big

A couple things are blurring the lines between being a marketer and an entrepreneur. It's actually got a lot to do with growing a brand, and whether that brand's a personal brand, a local business, your brand, a corporate global brand. I think the approach, remarkably, is the same.

You may be thinking "How does a marketer who is running a multi-million dollar budget and speaking to millions of people and growing a brand anything similar as far as strategies and tactics and challenges as me, the local business owner or me, the start-up entrepreneur?" The funny thing is, it is incredibly similar today. New media has completely changed the game. And in fact, I would say that more times than not, it's the start-ups, the entrepreneurs, the guys online who are in forums and just hustling like crazy that are on the leading edge. The marketers and agencies that are putting together these big programs are actually laggards in what's happening in the industry. So myself for example, how I've stayed sharp was getting knee-deep in what's happening on the forums, listening to podcasts, talking to people, reading books non-stop, going to conferences, non-stop engagement with the entrepreneur. It's those tactics brought over into global brands that have made the difference.

"New media has completely changed the game. It's the start-ups, the entrepreneurs who are just hustling like crazy that are on the leading edge. The marketers and agencies that are putting together these big programs are actually laggards in what's happening in the industry!"

A global brand will want to spend a ton of money. So you might have a $100 million brand, but you probably are spending $20 million on media. You're going to be doing TV, and doing all these sponsorships. Surprisingly, you can probably get a lot of reach and a lot of engagement and loyalty by doing things that entrepreneurs are doing today. For example, podcasts – you can do a podcast and reach potentially a billion people. We all know mobile devices are with everybody. You can't even have a conversation today with people without their head buried or their headphones in their ears, with a smart phone in their hand. That's the reality of today.

"Being small, being fast, being nimble is a competitive advantage."

It's very difficult for mass marketers, or medium-sized organizations as marketers to reach that audience. But you, the smaller, nimble entrepreneur have every equal opportunity. And in fact, it's almost an unfair advantage because you don't even have the restrictions. You don't have to put everything past the legal team because you don't have one. Or maybe you have a lawyer and just do some corporate stuff. There are a lot of advantages to being small. Like Seth Godin said, "Small is the new big." And there's a lot of truth to that. Being small, being fast, being nimble is a competitive advantage. And now, with new media, you're on a level playing field. It's entirely different. As a marketer, you have to understand this.

And you say, "Okay, how can I take advantage of new media?" So let's give an example: YouTube. YouTube is a huge platform. There are other video-sharing services out there too. We know about Vimeo – Vimeo has positioned itself as more of a premium tool, but you can use something like TubeMogal OneLoad, where you can upload, for a small fee, your video to TubeMogal OneLoad, and it actually distributes it to multiple video-sharing and hosting services: There's almost a dozen of them, including Vimeo and YouTube. So now you increase your exposure. So you can actually run a video – maybe it's a Q&A, maybe it's a little series you put together. You can host a YouTube live event or Google Hangouts or Skype or some sort of live webinar and then you publish that to TubeMogal, OneLoad out to all these distribution points online. You load the video with keywords, because YouTube is actually the second largest search engine, owned by Google. Everybody wants video; they don't even want to read anymore.

"YouTube is actually the second largest search engine, owned by Google. Everybody wants video; they don't even want to ready anymore. In fact, even premium video services such as Hulu can deliver great ROIs if you can afford them."

Did you know you can multi-purpose your video content across other platforms to get more juice out of it? You can convert video into a podcast, for example. And that podcast you can convert to a book, maybe an ebook. And maybe you can give that ebook away, or series away, for lead generation on your website. Maybe you want to publish it to Amazon. com and take advantage of their distribution network, which is a huge, huge lead generation tool for you. So if you put it on the Kindle network for 99¢, you can actually reach a new audience and use it for lead generation. Think about it. A majority of people start their product search on Amazon.com. and conversely a small percentage, start it on Google.

"Publish your content on Amazon.com to take advantage of their distribution network, which is a huge, huge lead generation tool for you... majority of product searches start today on Amazon, so you can get more than your fair share of eyeballs."

So if you're not on Amazon with your product, whether you're a small business, or even if you're offering a service – there's a way to get your service on there, think about that – or big business, you need to be there. That's where people are. Fish where the fish are. And you don't have to look at it to make money just on Amazon. Use it as a tool to build an audience, to reach people, to connect with them, to educate them, to build a relationship with them. They read your content, they see what you're about, and then they'll get warmed up to buy. Think about it as lead nurturing. It's just a process, we all go through it.

From there you can use those pieces of information to share it on social, share it on your blog, Facebook, Twitter, Instagram, Tumblr, you name it, even Pinterest. There are so many things that you can do. It's simple; it's so simple. And that's a completely level playing field if you're a small entrepreneur, or a consultant. You have a pool business or you have a brand worth $10 million, $20, $50, $100 million dollars – it doesn't make a difference. It's all the same. So that's why I think any sharp marketer is a sharp entrepreneur. And the two are interchangeable.

"Syndicate your content from your video to a podcast, to a book, to your website, to your social channels to save time and have a consistent message. After all, any sharp marketer is a sharp entrepreneur. The two are interchangeable."

Now you can use that to build a business and get some following, get some sales. And of course make sure you get a lead out of it. You bring them to your website to try to get a sale in there or tell them where to buy your product or service, how to get in touch with you. You have to make sure you always close that loop. Make sure you always have the sales funnel. Then eventually you can reach them with TV. You can actually do other videos that are commercial-oriented and put them on YouTube. And have a call to action and sell product through YouTube. Like TRX – that's what they did. They don't even do TV; they just used a YouTube direct response model. And that's a big brand that we know of. That's how the market has changed. You don't need to spend like the big boys, even if you are a big boy. Even though TV still has the best ROI at the date of this writing this book, the market has changed, but the opportunities are the same. It is probably the most disruptive and fragmented and equal opportune time for a young up-and-coming marketer, or an old dog. Or the entrepreneur who wants to get their message out there. It's absolutely unbelievable what's happening today for you to take advantage of.

> *"It is the most disruptive and fragmented and equal opportune time for a young up-and-coming marketer, old dog, or entrepreneur who wants to get their message out there. It's absolutely unbelievable what's happening today for you to take advantage of."*

And then of course you can still do other advertising, like radio. But if you have a podcast, you're basically on a radio show. Or maybe you want to advertise on a popular podcast. You reach out to a podcaster that has your target audience in mind, I bet you'd be surprised how cheap it is. And you can get multiple placements for pennies in comparison to radio. Now radio is good, radio is local and purchased properly can drive a handsome ROI. In fact, radio typically has the highest LTV of all other direct response vehicles because it reaches the consumer who is open to the message through their cerebral cortex and creative doesn't have to be updated for 18 months on average.

However, I never forget about email. Email is still the #1 killer app. Email has one of the highest ROIs of any tactical tool in the marketer's toolbox. Done properly, email can be almost a 50-1 ROI. If your email costs you $700 a year, you're looking at $35,000. So $35,000 in revenue off a $700 investment. Is that a good return? That's a great return! And that's what the typical costs are. If you get into something like Aweber, it's a little cheaper. If you get into something like MailChimp, it's a free trial to 500 members and then you can get up a bit higher than that. But there's a great opportunity there. These are tactical things that make a difference.

> *"Radio typically has the highest LTV of all other direct re-sponse vehicles, but email is still the #1 killer app. Done properly, email can be almost a 50:1 ROI."*

I started a dotcom business for a big global brand, so it was a new division and we only used email marketing, and minimal Google AdWords – I'm talking $1500 a month, whatever we could put on our corporate card. We built that up in a year to almost 250,000 email subscribers and a million dollars of revenue. A million dollars! Generating new content, putting videos up there, generating leads, communicating with email marketing, doing some AdWords. Believe it or not, this is back 10 years ago.

The game is even easier now, for anybody. So think about it. You don't have to go and spend an arm and a leg to be on an equal playing field with global brands. You are a small guy, you can absolutely compete. And if you're a big guy, you better look at the small guys. You better look to see what's happening out there – go to conferences, listen to podcasts, go online, look at forums, read books, stay sharp.

"If you're a big marketer, you better look at the small guys. You better look to see what's happening out there – go to conferences, listen to podcasts, go online, look at forums, read books, stay sharp – be humble because everybody is trying to get the edge."

That's how you're going to succeed and stay relevant. It's a new world order out there. It's so exciting, and yet so scary. And if you don't continuously evolve and look at what the trendsetters are doing, and look at what the new wave of innovation is, you're going to be in trouble. If you're just getting into Google AdWords now, you're going to be paying too much. You should be looking at Facebook ads. Facebook ads are half the cost per acquisition, cost per click. And they're more targeted than Google AdWords.

So food for thought, lots to think about. Things are changing. Face fear. Try it. Put yourself out there. Put yourself in front of a video camera. Put yourself in front of a microphone. Make it happen.

Chapter 5

Niche vs. Mass

There are a lot of insights that you can learn from this book, just on the fringes of marketing, not even necessarily in the masses. It really comes down to positioning. What I want to share here and now is to go mass or to go niche and expose the lure of each of them and where you should go to build *your* brand.

> *"It really comes down to positioning, then… to go mass or to go niche and the lure of each of them and where you should go to build your brand."*

So this is an interesting topic because let's be honest, there is a significant lure and attraction to the mass market. I think it's every marketer's and entrepreneur's dream to be able to see their product on the shelves of Walmart, Target, and other leading mass retailers. I mean that is a major accomplishment. I've had the luxury of pitching products to Walmart headquarters, sitting across the table from the buyer and telling the brand story, telling why it's so unique, telling them how much margin they're going to make, how much money they're going to make, what you anticipate the units per store per week metric to be, the marketing campaign, the creative, all that kind of stuff, how we're going to partner with them, the freestanding inserts we're going to do with them, the in-store PDQs and promotions we're going to do, and how we're going to make them a destination, and a market leader, and all that kind of stuff. And they love it. Why? They get to make money! And you get to make money. They're a beast to work with, but we do love them because of their massive scale.

I've sold in more products than I can count at Walmart and, with of course a great sales team, built the marketing plan and sales deck to help sell in it and sell it through for somewhere close to a billion dollars in sales over the last 15 years.

That takes a lot of work. They bring with them a big challenge. So a mass market item is amazing for so many reasons, because, of course, it's everywhere. It's ubiquitous. But with it comes a price. That price really is building awareness. So if you have a new product and you're marketing it, and it's a mass product, how are you going to get that awareness out there fast enough to drive retail turns, sales? And so therein lies the challenge.

"A mass market item is amazing for so many reasons, because of course, it's everywhere... but it comes with a price. That price is building awareness... fast enough to drive retail turns."

So if you're creating a brand and you have the opportunity to think mass or niche, I would urge you to go niche. Why? You can actually create a meaningful product. I find that when a product goes mass, it loses its identity. You know what I mean? For example it's chewing gum, ok great, it's chewing gum. Or it's liquid detergent or it's something like…

a consumable product that is really just not exciting. It's targeting a mother of two who's married or what have you, just kind of standard thing that really isn't exciting. You don't really have a strong persona. Plus, the kicker is you usually have to be in all this media in order to reach your audience.

"I would urge you to go niche… you can actually create a meaningful product. I find that when a product goes mass, it loses its identity."

But when you go niche, it allows you as the entrepreneur or marketer to be very, very focused in your marketing messages. So you're not appealing to everybody. You probably don't have the mass market opportunity for distribution. But what it gives you is a very focused opportunity. An example would be if you're selling an energy bar. You're selling an energy bar and you know that you can sell this to convenience channel. And a young guy will probably stop at a convenience store, so that's an opportunity for distribution. You probably could get it into mass market, but that'll take a lot of challenge and there's slim margins there. You can get it into online retailers.

"When you go niche, it allows you to be very focused in your marketing messages… what it gives you is a very focused opportunity for distribution."

But what if you said "Okay, who really is the consumer for this?" And maybe you decided, alright, it is an energy bar and I'm going to target towards bodybuilders. You're not going to target extreme weekend warriors; you're not going to target the endurance athletes. You're going to target bodybuilders. Maybe you want to make this a bit unique and it's going to have a little bit of creatine in it for muscle building. So it's an energy bar that also has a muscle builder built into it. So now you've defined your audience a little more specifically. Then you decided "Okay great, this is what I'm going to do. I'm going to go after the bodybuilders' segment."

Then you have to ask yourself what distribution is going to make sense and how you're going to launch that. Well, I would urge you to go in something that is very niche, yet has good distribution and be able to get immediate response. So, for example, bodybuilding.com – bodybuilding.com is the largest online resource for bodybuilders and fitness enthusiasts. You can actually get a significant point of distribution, actually even access international markets. I've worked with bodybuilding.com before, and they're a great organization out of Boise, Idaho. Amazon recently has made major moves to take share away from Bodybuilding.com, so that too would be another sales channel.

Now you have an energy bar and could have went mass with it, but then decided to make it a little more niche. You wanted to make it focused on bodybuilders. Now you've identified bodybuilding.com as the customer you want to go after. And maybe what you do is an exclusivity deal with them, and say "Okay, you can get this bar only at bodybuilding.com" so it gives bodybuilding.com the opportunity to get behind it as a product or a brand. It allows you the marketer or the entrepreneur to go there and say "Okay, now I can focus all my effort, very focused, laser focused on this platform, on this distribution partner, on a retailer who wants to build this product with me."

> *"With focus you can do an exclusivity deal. It gives the retailer the opportunity to get behind your product or brand and you can be laser focused on making it a success with them and your target audience."*

Then you can go and do promotions with bodybuilding.com – maybe buy one get one free, maybe do sampling on every order that goes out.

And they ship out 100,000 orders a month. You can do programs for pay per click to drive traffic to the page to buy there. You can put it on shopping feeds, on Google Shopping and drive it to bodybuilding.com to get the sale. You can build an email list, and drive it to bodybuilding.com to get the sale. And then you can maybe partner with other brands. If somebody buys their product, they get 50% off your bar or something like that, or vice versa. You can be extremely focused on that segment and on that retailer. All your funds go towards that; all your energy goes towards that. And you can have success. And then that success there – once you're one thing to one audience and one retail partner, you can have dramatic success because it's all about the laser focus of your advertising dollars, of your effort, of your relationships, and your retailer performance.

Ultimately, that allows you to get a success at a retailer, and then bring your product to other ones after that exclusivity is over. Versus trying to go everywhere all at once and spread your dollars thin.

"After you get success at a retailer, bring your product to other ones after that exclusivity is over. Versus trying to go everywhere all at once and spread your dollars thin."

If you wanted to reach all fitness enthusiasts age 25-65 who might be interested in you bar. If you went mass market and only did advertising online through Google, for example… that's about 150 million people you'd have to reach, it would take you roughly $8 million. $8 million to reach that audience enough times in a matter of 5, 6 months to get enough impression, to get a recall rate to impact sales and sell thru. So you're really diluting your dollars. Yeah, there's a lure there to get some money in and "Wow, we got great distribution. High five." But it's a very slippery slope too, because you need a lot of money to win. You'll probably end up just being on TV if you can afford it and you'll just burn money. Or you'll try events maybe, and sampling, but will that be enough to drive the trial, to get enough units per store per week metrics?

"To reach a mass audience enough times... to get a recall rate to impact sales and sell thru, you're really diluting your dollars and you need a lot of money to win... you'll probably end up on TV if you can afford it."

Then you'll try spending in-store and quickly realize why you can't spend all the money in-store. These are challenges that marketers and entrepreneurs face. And a lot of you as entrepreneurs might think "Wow, I can only dream of having that problem. I have a product I'm only selling on my own store. Or I'm doing an information product." Those are things to think about as an illustration of focus and not to get greedy, to think you want all the distribution in the world, immediately. You really have to think about phased, focused marketing and sales.

You know some of the best brands ever built have done this – start off focused on a very specific niche. Own the niche, and that niche will bleed over into other markets allowing you to grow naturally with that, with those markets and that brand, having a very efficient and high return on ad spend. You can be very focused on what you need to do.

"Some of the best brands ever built have started off focused on a very specific niche. Own the niche, and that niche will bleed over into other markets allowing you to grow naturally."

If you look at Vans, which is a well-known brand that started off in the skating community. They focused on skaters and now you can see 65-year-old men wearing a pair of Vans they got at Walmart. They went mass market eventually, but not until they really owned a niche. And they owned that niche of skateboarding back in the '90s. I mean, I grew up with that. DC Shoes was also in the same category. However, they've stayed a little more to the core. But Vans is an excellent example. And as you get more mass, you get more pressure on margins, so you have to make the product less effective and cut some corners to reduce costs. It's all about saving pennies because you're working on huge volumes now. But when you're going a bit smaller and you're focused, you can focus on extreme product quality, extremely powerful relationships, not only at the retail level, but also at the consumer level. And it really allows you to maximize your effort, which is the biggest advantage.

If you're just starting out and you're looking at launching a product or a service or an information product, really be careful about how you're positioning, who you're targeting. And then another component is to really think about your distribution. If you're offering an information product, for example. I've done this before – a health and fitness product. I could have easily gone to all the affiliate networks, could have put it everywhere, just do the spaghetti strategy (throw a bunch of stuff at the wall and see what sticks). The spaghetti strategy is important in some ways – it does work when you're initially trying to find a partner. But if I just went everywhere and spread myself so thin without partnering with ClickBank for example and really trying to figure out ClickBank, I would have gotten nowhere. There's JVZoo, there is ShareASale, I've talked about all these different affiliate networks before. But if you just say "Okay, ClickBank is the biggest. It has the most information products. It has the best marketplace right now. Yeah, there are fees, yeah, there's a little learning curve, but I'm going to focus on ClickBank. I'm going to try to figure out everything I can about ClickBank. I'm going to try to own that platform. I'm going talk to people who are successful on that platform. I'm going to take my lumps on that platform. And I'm really going to crack the code on it. I'm going to own it. I'm going to be successful. And I'm not going to quit until I win."

"The spaghetti strategy in important in some ways – it does work when you're initially trying to find a partner. But if I just went everywhere and spread myself so thin without partnering with ClickBank, I would have gotten nowhere."

Eventually, you may want to quit it, you've just done everything you can, and a mentor told you it's not going to make it because maybe you messed up your price or whatever. But the point is you really want to point your effort and your interest at one thing. Master it. Monetize it. Learn from it. Focus your energy and your dollars at it. That's where you get your return. Then look at expanding your effort and your dollars beyond that. So that's a very important lesson. Lots of time we talk about focus from the perspective of your business and your priorities as far as developing new products or different business ventures. Now I'm asking you to focus on your distribution and your marketing. And if you do it, you'll find that you'll have excellent success.

"Point your effort and your interest at one thing. Master it. Monetize it. Learn from it. Focus your energy and your dollars at it."

You can see the benefits of niche. That's where to start. Don't get too greedy upfront. I've seen businesses fail as a result of it. I can't tell you enough. You'll get there. You'll eventually get to where you want to go. It is a journey. Be patient. Be something amazing to a retailer, a partner, a distribution partner, a platform, a customer, and trust me, it'll come back to you a hundredfold. You'll grow. You'll prosper. You'll have a little more time and less stress. You'll be a better person for it.

Chapter 6

Control Your Health for Wealth

've had the blessed fortune of being involved in the health and wellness and fitness industry for the last 25 years. My journey started out, actually when I was 16, when I picked up my first weight and started working out. By the age of 18, I did my first bodybuilding show. And that was really a drive to have a healthy body, to be fit, and where that stemmed from, in retrospect I believe, was when I was a kid. As a kid I was overweight. I was so overweight, my family and I joked around, that I couldn't wear jeans. I only could wear jogging pants because I needed the elastic in the waist. I was always the tall kid and the big kid. And I wasn't like the kid in *The Goonies* who does the truffle shuffle. I wasn't like that, but nonetheless I was a big kid.

My nutrition wasn't great. I had a great appetite, I ate a lot, but I wasn't very active. And I sat in front of the Commodore 64 playing video games, I was eating potato chips and drinking soda. A lot of starch, a lot of pasta, and everything – I just wasn't healthy. I was healthy when I was really young, because my mother forced me to eat a lot of locally grown organic food. She had her own garden so she always put out vegetables and we had everything from a farm. I was very blessed to have good nutrients from a very young age, but as I got a bit older – 8, 9, 10,

11, 12, and so on – I just got lazy, and I really enjoyed all the junk foods and the video games back in the day.

> *"I sat in front of the Commodore 64 playing video games, I was eating potato chips and drinking soda. I just wasn't healthy."*

It wasn't until I felt really bad about myself, I felt so bad about myself, I think it really impacted me psychologically. I developed a stutter. Sometimes I got very nervous around people because I just wasn't confident. I felt really insecure. I think that's what drove me when I got into my teenage years, and I really grew a lot. I grew up to about 6'1" and was about 165 pounds when I was about 14 years old. So I was tall, slim, I was athletic. I started working out when I was about 16, got really hooked on it. And then at age 18, I was so involved in it, a friend of mine and I got together and said, "Let's do a bodybuilding show." So I started doing supplementation, and meal replacement shakes, eating really clean. And at that point, I was bigger, I was 212 lbs. And I went down to 175 in 6 months; the leanest I've ever been. I did my body building show and I didn't place, I didn't win, but that's okay – I felt like I had a big victory.

> *"I started working out when I was about 16, got really hooked on it. I started doing supplementation, and meal replacement shakes, eating clean. I did my bodybuilding show and I didn't place, I didn't win, but that's okay – I felt like I had a big victory."*

The reality is that it actually wasn't that healthy either. I was cutting water, only drinking distilled water in the end, carb-loading on potatoes. I mean all these crazy things you do. But what it taught me was a very valuable lesson – that food is a powerful drug. So other people might say, "Well it's information for your body. It really is nourishment and then the end result is your body is like the receipt of what you put into it." I always view it as food is a drug because it's a very literal sense to me, you know, there's a results-oriented component where I put something in and something happens. Like a drug – you take a drug for a symptom and then there's a benefit. So what it taught me was that food is a powerful drug. That it's more powerful than training, it's more powerful than sleep. It really is nourishment for the soul so you can operate at a higher level.

> *"Food is a powerful drug. It's more powerful than training, it's more powerful than sleep. It really is nourishment for the soul so you can operate at a higher level."*

In order for you to operate at your peak performance, where you feel like you're in the zone, you've got the flow going on, you're totally focused – which, focusing today is very hard – and you feel like you can conquer anything, you really need to be optimized. There's really three main pillars for physical health. There is nutrition, there is sleep, and there is exercise. So in my life, I really focus on those three things, and have had a lifelong passion for learning and trying to optimize those all the time.

> *"To operate at your peak performance… there's really three main pillars for physical health. There is nutrition, there is sleep, and there is exercise."*

As mentioned I did my first show at 18, ended up managing a health food store when I was 20, and that did very well. I learned a ton there. Later on I started a job with one of the world's leading supplement companies and that's where I had the luxury of building #1 brands. During that time I learned a lot of how different nutrients impact the body, and the timing of the nutrients, all the different training principles, and I was working with the top trainers in the world. Then doing transformations with people who are really overweight, and tweaking their diets and working with fitness and nutrition experts to transform men and women's bodies who would lose like 80 lbs., 50 lbs., 30 lbs., and do it in a healthy way, look good, and feel good.

> *"I started a job with one of the world's leading supplement companies and that's where I had the luxury of building #1 brands. During that time I learned a lot of how different nutrients impact the body."*

And what I saw was something incredible, just so incredibly rewarding. People felt like they were victims, that they were a byproduct of the bad luck that they received. These people were overweight, they had relationship issues, they had challenges in their career. They felt like it was desperation time for them. They just were "poor me," they weren't having success. And what happened was as soon as you take responsibility and take action and understand the impact of nutrition, sleep, and exercise, and the role it plays in your body, something profound happens.

> *"As soon as you take responsibility and take action and understand the impact of nutrition, sleep, and exercise, and the role it plays in your body, something profound happens."*

What happens is every element in your life changes for the positive. You take responsibility, you take action, and you make change. I've seen it so many times, hundreds of people that, all of a sudden, they get out of a bad relationship, all of a sudden they get a promotion in their career, or they change careers, or they start their own business, they become an advocate for something, they get involved socially in the community, they pursue a lifelong dream. Why? They are finally optimized for health. They are vibrant, they have the energy, they look good, they feel good, they are in control of their body, and what goes in their body. Think about that for a minute.

"Every element in your life changes for the positive. You take responsibility, you take action, and you make change."

Wouldn't you like to feel like you're in complete control of your health, and your wealth? There is a saying that health is the new wealth. I think there's a lot of truth to that – if you're controlling your health, you have the absolute best opportunities to control your wealth. As a high-performing entrepreneur and a high performing executive, you really need to optimize it. Cut out the coffees, cut out the donuts, cut out the crap. Focus on the good stuff. Now, I will say I drink coffee. I drink coffee every morning. I actually have an Americano every morning, but I use organic fair trade coffee, not only is it ethical, but I believe you try to put good things in your body as much as possible. Even if coffee isn't all that good. It is a drug, caffeine is a drug. Try to put the best sources you can in there. I limit my consumption to probably two cups a day. And I don't consume coffee after about roughly 2:00, 3:00pm. And why is that?

Well, in launching an energy drink before, I did a lot of research on caffeine, and there's a lot of clinical studies on the impact of caffeine. Basically, caffeine has a half-life. If you've got 300 mg of caffeine in a strong coffee – and I think you know what kind of brand I'm talking about – well several hours later, there's going to be about 150 mg in your body. It's going to disrupt your sleeping behavior. It definitely impacts your central nervous system. There definitely is an impact there to your body. So you want to manage it. You want to be aware of it, and then once you're armed with information you want to manage it. What I do is, I just take it earlier on, 2:00pm at the latest.

Tangent: As I was creating this content for the book I was interrupted with a phone call. I had a very close family member pass away due to poor health. I think it puts things into perspective. Not only is optimal health important for performance and focus and your success at your career, but it also is important for longevity. It's important for your family, so you can give all you can to your family, so you can be in the moment, you can be vibrant and healthy and happier and be able to give more of yourself to those that you love, that you want to serve because, let's face it, our time on earth is limited. It really is, and there's only so many moments that are available to us, that we need to really seize. If you're in poor health, it's very difficult to do that. Not only is optimal health important for your career, but oh man, it is absolutely necessary to live a fuller life. That's my main message to you. With that said, I want to move on to the rest of this good stuff.

> *"Optimal health… it's important for your family, so you can give all you can to your family, so you can be in the moment, you can be vibrant and healthy and happier and be able to give more of yourself to those that you love."*

What can you do, right? "Okay, great, Darren, you've talked about how health is important. I get it. Now what can I do?" Well, what can you do? There's a lot of different things. So we talked about the three pillars: we talked about exercise, about nutrition, and sleep. So let's talk about sleep, #1. Sleep is when your body repairs itself. You push it through the day and at night, it recovers. For example bodybuilders always spoke of eating and sleeping. Everybody was saying: "Oh, I got to get my 8 hours of sleep, I got to get 9 hours of sleep. I got to take my branch chain amino acid before going to bed. Or slow-release protein so I get a steady influx of amino acids so I don't have catabolism at night, which is muscle wasting."

Now, I don't think the average person needs to do that. However, what you need is that 8 hours of sleep. I mean, you really need to get that deep sleep. There's apps out there to help you. I don't recommend those apps and the reason being is you probably shouldn't have your device around you when you're trying to go to bed, whether it's an alarm clock or however you use it. I'm guilty of it – I've used mine as an alarm clock for years, but I've made a conscious effort to just kind of tuck that away. There's a lot of radiation. You can get attachments and devices to your device that reduces radiation if you're concerned and can't turn it off. There is a lot of evidence that suggests that sleeping near your device is really bad for your health, in relation to tumors, brain tumors, breast tumors. So the best thing to do is just avoid that so you can ensure you have a great sleep.

> **"Sleep is when your body repairs itself… get 8 hours of deep sleep."**

The second thing is to make sure your room is quiet. No TV, no radios, those kinds of things. You really want to have a quiet area. The third thing is you want to have darkness. You want it to be nice and dark. So what happens is… and I did a lot of research on this when I was working on a sleep product I brought to market. What I learned about was the circadian rhythm and how everybody has a circadian rhythm. And that's really your sleep-wake cycle. You wake up in the morning, maybe it's at 7:00, you wake up and then you have a burst of energy and then you kind of dip down a bit mid-day, maybe 2:00, 3:00, and then you rally back and then you get tired maybe around 10:00. That's your circadian rhythm, and you know it's really out of whack especially when you travel. When you travel from east to west and west to east, when you go through those different time zones, that impacts your circadian rhythm. Now all of a sudden your internal clock is off because the daylight is tricking your body and saying, "Woah, woah, woah, that's not what I'm used to seeing. Okay, I'm going to stay up later." And then everything's off. So when you travel, even try to stay in that same sleep pattern if you can because it will help you when you get back to your home time zone. Your circadian rhythm… here's something very interesting, you want to try to regulate it as much as possible. It's very hormonal. There's a hormone called melatonin that helps regulate that, and a lot of sleep products contain melatonin to regulate your sleep-wake cycle and your circadian rhythm.

> *"Everyone has a circadian rhythm… your sleep-wake cycle.*
> *You want to regulate it as much as possible."*

There are ways to help your natural circadian rhythm: 1) Go to bed at the same time every day. 2) Get up at the same time every day. That includes weekends. So, that's what I've done, whether it's the weekend or the weekday, it doesn't matter. I get up the same time. You'll find, and what I've found, is you wake up before your alarm clock. Eyes wide open, maybe 2 minutes, 5 minutes before your alarm clock. What a beautiful way to wake up because your body is saying: "Yup, that's the rhythm. That's the right thing to do." You feel rested. You got your REM sleep because your room was dark. You didn't have any devices going on. It's quiet. It's very consistent.

It's really important – get that sleep. You can survive on 6 hours, 4 hours, whatever, but really the best thing for your health is to get that 8. 7-9 hours is what they say, but 8 hours is a good thing to shoot for. If you're going to bed at 10:00 pm, you're getting up at 6:00; if you're going to bed at 11:00, you're getting up at 7:00. So that's something to consider. Get consistent sleep. You'll feel a lot better, you won't be irritable, and you'll probably even look better.

Next is nutrition. In the mornings, I usually have a smoothie and mix it up for variety. This one in particular, has cinnamon – and cinnamon has a high ORAC value, which is antioxidant value. So if you're unsure what ORAC is, Google ORAC values, and you can see it has all the antioxidants. Cinnamon is top of the charts, way more antioxidants, free radical killers than pretty much anything else. People say "What about acai? I heard that's great. What about blueberries?" Cinnamon dwarfs it. Not only does cinnamon have the highest ORAC value of many ingredients out there, natural substances, but it also has a natural thermogenic component to it. So what is thermogenesis?

"Nutrition… have a smoothie. Cinnamon has a high ORAC value… way more antioxidants, free radical killers than pretty much anything else. It also has a natural thermogenic component to it."

Thermogenesis is really when your body heats up to burn energy. Additionally, what you'll find is if you continue to take cinnamon, not only does it help with thermogenesis, but it also helps with insulin sensitivity. Cinnamon: a very powerful antioxidant, very good for your health, very good if you're trying to lose weight, and of course it tastes pretty good.

I also put in almond butter. So typically I don't eat peanut butter and the reason why I don't eat peanut butter is simply because, well, here's a story, and for those of you who know the facts, by all means tweet me or message me about this. Peanuts are the source for peanut butter. Typically what happens is that all the leftover peanuts that don't make it to the bag for consumption as peanuts go to peanut butter. That may not be the case for all manufacturers of peanut butter, but definitely for the larger manufacturers. There is a byproduct in those peanuts called aflatoxin and it's very unhealthy for you. It is not recommended obviously for consumption. I just stay away from it. What I do is I use sources like almond butter to give that sweetness, that flavor. Almonds are great for you. Get organic if you can.

> *"Peanut butter… there is a byproduct in those peanuts called aflatoxin and it's very unhealthy for you. I just stay away from it. I use sources like almond butter."*

I don't use any sugars, or I don't put any juices in the shakes, nothing like that. I just add water. Sometimes organic almond milk because I don't eat dairy. The odd time I'll have Greek yogurt. But dairy and man-made wheat and processed stuff is not good. So that's the shake. It's a nice quick thing to have, takes five minutes if that, and you're super-charged for the morning, you're very focused.

Then also what I take is fish oils. So to put it into perspective, there are – last I checked – about 334, I think, probably more, clinical studies on fish oil. Not just the fish oil itself, but the compounds, the active compounds called EPA and DHA – you might have heard that before. The ratio typically of EPA to DHA in most fish oils is 180 over 120. And you can get different ratios based on what it is you're looking for. There's a lot of studies on EPA-DHA ratios and amounts. Whether that's for heart health, joint health, anti-inflammatory properties, ocular health, for improving vision believe it or not, I believe it's related to glaucoma. There are studies on brain activity and mental acuity, focus, cholesterol, triglycerides, and heart health.

> *"I take fish oils. The ratio typically of EPA to DHA in most fish oils is 180 over 120. There's a lot of studies on EPA-DHA ratios and amounts."*

As you can see it's very important to take a good quality fish oil. I would look at label that has *Meg3* as a source of fish oil – it's a very good, cost-effective pure source of fish oil. So a lot of different brands use *Meg3* and it looks like a little fish on the back of the label. There are other really powerful, effective fish oils if you're willing to spend the money. Supercritical fish oil – there's only 2 companies in the world that make this. One is in Spain, the other in the US. Typically what happens is when you buy a fish oil of 180:120 EPA:DHA, you get about 1000 mgs in a big fish oil soft gel. Out of that 1000 mg, only 300 of that is active –180 and 120 is 300. So 30% of that is active. Supercritical on the other hand is up to 90% of active ingredients – the EPA/DHA – and only 10% of the oil is just the waste. It's inefficient. What that means is you get less of the inactive, and more of the active. So you can take 1 of those and it will be many times more effective than standard fish oil.

You should really just try to eat whole foods as well. Processed foods, quick and easy, drive-through, all that kind of stuff is not ideal for you. Whole foods are ideal. A simple rule of thumb is when you're shopping, shop the outer aisle of the grocery store. That's where the produce is, that's where the healthy foods are, that's where the meat is, that's where you need to be. All the inner aisles are typically man-made processed stuff. Those have additives in it, preservatives that are really foreign to our body. Ideally try not to put anything foreign in your body. We're talking optimal health, this is focused, this is performance, and everything for your success.

> *"Try to eat whole foods. A simple rule of thumb is when you're shopping, shop the outer aisle of the grocery store."*

Put in good, nutrient dense foods. That's what it comes down to, it's all about the nutrients you put in your body. If you look at food, as I said before as a drug, as a fuel, what ingredients, what fuel, what drugs are you putting in your body? Are you putting in sulphites and preservatives and nitrates? Are you putting in things that you just can't even pronounce? Are you putting in red dyes? What are you doing to your body? And a lot of the evidence of these ingredients haven't even been proven how it impacts your health in the long term. There's a lot of studies on ingredients of course, and they have to pass safety thresholds of course by governing bodies in order to be put into food, and the food supply, but long term, the effects are questionable.

> *"Look at food as a drug. What ingredients, what fuel, what drugs are you putting in your body? Are you putting in things that you just can't even pronounce?"*

If you are one of those people with a sweet tooth, I'd recommend get away from white refined sugar, get away from artificial sweeteners like aspartame, xylitol, maltitol, ace k, etc. You can do your own research on it, but stevia is a plant-based sweetener that has a low glycemic index so it's not going to bump up insulin response. If somebody is diabetic for example, it would be a good alternative for them. I know it's a challenge for them to find something that has some sweetness to it that is decent for their health.

> *"Get away from refined sugar... get away from artificial sweeteners... but stevia is a plant-based sweetener that has a low glycemic index so it's not going to bump up insulin response."*

There's other sources out there too. You can even go to yacon syrup, low glycemic index if you really want to get something really healthy. Stevia is very, very good. You could use honey... honey, there's a lot of benefits to honey, but honey has a lot of high fructose, so if you can use stevia and you just need a little bit and you can put it in your coffee and whatever you want. Although watch your coffee consumption as mentioned earlier.

I bet you're thinking: "Okay Darren, great, I shop in the outer aisle, I eat whole foods, greens, veggies, all that kind of stuff. So how do I break it down? How often do I eat? What do I eat exactly?" Well #1, I'm not a nutritionist but I've been in the industry for over 20 years now. Transforming people and transforming my own body and competing in multiple bodybuilding shows and losing a bunch of weight and understanding what works and seeing what works for other people. It's all about the results. Plus, I've had the good fortune of working with nutritionists, some of the best in the industry.

> *"I've had the good fortune of working with nutritionists, some of the best in the industry."*

With greens, typically you can really eat as much as you want. With the fruits, frankly, my perspective is I try to eat a lot of fruits. If I'm eating two apples a day, I'm having my berries in the morning. If I feel like I want some berries later on in the day, like midday, I'll have some. I'm not going to restrict myself because it's not really all that calorie dense. I try not to have really sweet fruit because it's so high in sugar.

> *"Greens, typically you can really eat as much as you want. Fruits, frankly, my perspective is I try to eat a lot of fruits… I try not to have really sweet fruit because it's so high in sugar."*

Typically what I try to do is balance out insulin levels with fats. I mentioned the fish oil before, but look at healthy fats. Avocados – can you combine avocado with your meal? What it's going to do, it's going to slow your insulin spike. It's going to really manipulate it, slow it down so you don't get that huge rush of sugar and then the crash. Nice level energy going on there. Nuts – so almonds, cashews, walnuts, even Brazil nuts, so those are good sources of fats. I try to combine fats with every meal so I can have a nice steady state of insulin response. Nice and regulated – that's what I look at.

> *"You can combine fats with every meal… to have a nice steady state of insulin response."*

Now protein, protein is great for satiety and loaded with amino acids to actually help you fuel your body. It's the growth, it'll help your muscles grow/recover and be sustained. I try to have protein every meal as well, just a little bit, probably 20, 30 grams, so maybe that's a chicken breast, maybe that's a piece of fish. Beef, probably once a week, maybe twice a week – try to get grass-fed if you can. Find a butcher that can do that or a farmer and go in with somebody and maybe split a side of beef. Just find good sources. Eggs, eggs are great. Eggs are great in the morning or as a snack later on. You can hard boil those things and then have them later on in the day as a nice healthy snack.

> *"Protein is great for satiety and loaded with amino acids to actually help fuel your body… it'll help your muscles grow/recover and be sustained."*

Typically what I do is, the rule of thumb is I try to eat every few hours. So in the morning, I'll wake up, I'll eat, I'll have my smoothie. I'll have a snack around 2-3 hours later. It might be an apple, some nuts, maybe I'll have an egg or something like that. And then I'll have my lunch. My lunch, I typically have a salad with more greens. I might have a sweet potato – sweet potato is fine, by the way. It's not really starch like a regular potato, which is loaded with sugar. It has a ton of nutrients. Then a protein source whether that's going to be a piece of chicken, fish, what have you. That's my lunch. Later on in the afternoon, I might have maybe a little bit of berries with maybe another apple. I might grab a little protein shake if that's what I want. Then I'll go have dinner. Dinner, again, very similar to my lunch, another salad, more veggies, maybe it's asparagus, maybe it's broccoli, whatever. A source of protein again; chicken, fish, pork, or beef. Then the fats – I will either have a handful of nuts or I'll put those nuts in my salads. Or lots of times what I do is I take my fish oils again, so that'll balance out my fat consumption there. Typically, that's what I do. And later on in the evening if I'm still hungry, I might have some hummus with some celery as an example.

If you look at it from a macronutrient perspective – macronutrients are your proteins, your carbohydrates, your fats – the rule of thumb is roughly 1 gram of protein for every pound of lean body mass to maintain the lean body mass that you have today. So say, you're 200 lbs. and you have 170 lbs. of lean muscle mass. And you can go to your local gym and ask for a caliper test, or maybe use the BOD POD or something like that, to get your body fat measured so you understand what's your lean mass and what is your body fat.

> *"The rule of thumb is roughly 1 gram of protein for every pound of lean body mass to maintain the lean body mass that you have today."*

So you'll find that out and say it's 170. So you should have roughly 170 g of protein a day. And you can divide that up by how many meals you have a day. So whether that's 5 meals a day, 4 meals, you just do the math. So say it's 5, you're roughly having 30-ish g of protein a meal. Then you're having carbs, you probably want to have 1-1.5 grams of carbs per pound of lean body mass. Like I said earlier, your carb sources should be greens, you can have sweet potatoes if you like. Really just try to limit your man-made starches as much as possible. And then for fat, it's about .3, so .3 grams per pound of your lean body mass. So in this case, we're looking at 40 grams of fat. You want to have that kind of mix as much as possible in your meals. So that's my take on nutrition. If you have any questions or anything, you can just shoot me a tweet. I would be happy to respond to you and give you a little insight more of what I do, and what I've seen work and be effective. And by the way, I've seen this… it's uncanny the results that people get. They feel great, they feel empowered, they get back to their optimum health, the weight just comes off, they have more energy. It's a great thing to see. It's a great transformation.

> *"Carbs, you probably want to have 1 – 1.5 grams of carbs per pound of lean body mass. Fat, it's about .3 grams per pound of your lean body mass."*

Then it comes down to exercise. A lot of people think "Well, I work out, I can eat whatever I want." Well, yeah, if you're 15 years old! As our hormones change as we get older, you'll find that whatever you eat now, just like, "Oh man, I can't eat as much. I'm full right away. Plus, it just seems to go to my hips or my arms or my belly," or whatever that so-called trouble spot is for you. And that has to do with your hormonal levels.

Exercise doesn't have to be hours a day. If you're a busy person like myself, you got a lot of things on the go, what I found works is really high intensity training. If you're just starting out, I don't recommend it. You have to kind of build up to it. This is what I do because I've been working out for years. I will go probably about 20 minutes, 30 minutes of maximum output on a workout, and it's usually a metabolic conditioning workout, meaning I don't take any rests, I just power through.

It'll be air squats, maybe wall ball tosses, it might be lunges, it might be push-ups, sit-ups, pull-ups, a lot of body weight stuff. Then I'll do rounds of exercises, such as a 400 meter run. If I really want to get in shape and get a good workout in there, I will incorporate some strength movements maybe once or twice a week, whether that's deadlifts, squats to really stimulate the production of growth hormone to maintain my muscle mass.

"Our hormones change as we get older… Exercise doesn't have to be for hours a day. What I found works is high intensity training for metabolic conditioning."

Metabolic conditioning is a great intense workout. You get a sweat immediately. You get your heart rate up there. It's aerobic and anaerobic. So say I do the 400 meter run, I might do 10, 15 chin-ups, I might do 20 push-ups, let's say I'm going to do 10 air squats. And I'm going to do 3 rounds of that, or 4 rounds of that, or 5 rounds of that depending on how energetic I am that day, for time. How fast can I do it? And I'll warm up a bit – I'll do a light jog, I'll do some stretching. And afterwards I'll cool down and I'll stretch out just to avoid some injuries, maintain flexibility and overall health. And you know, mobility is really important, especially as you get older.

What I've found is that the weight just peels off, my cardiovascular health is great, my strength is maintained, I feel good, I got my sweat, the serotonin level is elevated, the endorphins are elevated, I feel like I got my nice natural high, stress is down. That allows me to focus more on what I have to do and give more to my family. To give more to my career, and the podcast, and everything else that I have going on. Then incorporating some strength movements… if you're a woman reading this and you're thinking "Oh, I would never do deadlifts, I would never do squats with weights" guess what – you're not going to get big and bulky, okay.

It's not going to happen. You're a woman; you're still going to look like a woman. You're going to be as beautiful as ever. You're going to be a little more toned, have a little more muscle definition. And frankly, strong is the new sexy. There's a big movement going on – women can be strong, women can have good conditioning, just like a man. But you'll look like a woman – just a fit woman. There's nothing to worry about there.

> *"High intensity training works great for men and women to help shed off the weight and keep your muscles toned. Women won't become bulky, but instead look and feel fit and healthy."*

High intensity interval training is also another great thing to check out. It's very much metabolic conditioning. If you want to do classes and things like that, more of the high impact, check them out. I recommend CrossFit; as you can see, much of what I described sounds like CrossFit. I'm an advocate. I also recommend checking out some resources online – there's a lot of them. There's websites like BodyRocker.tv, videos on YouTube, Zuzka – she's great, you can follow her – Zuzka Light. She's got great information on bodyweight exercise, and if you're travelling the workouts are easy to follow along with in your hotel room. There's a lot of opportunities for you to get in shape. And it doesn't take long – 20, 30 minutes, sometimes it's even 15 minutes. And if you can do that 3, 4, even 5 times a week, which is not a lot of time, you can do this. You'll be in control of your body, of your mind, and be able to give optimum performance.

I hope there's something that you took away from this chapter, and understand the relationship of your health – what you put in your body, how much sleep you get, keeping that body active and mobile – and how that impacts your overall health, performance, and longevity, and ultimately your happiness and success in life.

Section 2

It's Time to Build a Marketing Machine

Chapter 7

The Secret to Creating #1 Selling Products

There's a huge opportunity in front of you right now, and I'm really fired up about this. There are two ways, I think, that you can bring products to market, or identify what the product concept is. That is, you can identify something that is a little bit different, like the blue ocean strategy, which would be creating something that is uniquely positioned, differentiated, and has a new category. So you're a category creator. Everybody loves category creators; however, it takes a lot of money and effort to really succeed. But when you do, you can enjoy the market opportunity for as long as it takes for a competitor to copy you. And we already know that the way to insulate yourself from competition is through experience, to provide an experience that no other brand can.

> *"Everybody loves category creators; however, it takes a lot of money and effort to really succeed. But when you do, you can enjoy the market opportunity for as long as it takes for a competitor to copy you."*

But the real purpose is to explain to you how to develop a product or a service to be one of the top sellers, fast. If your goal is identify what is the #1 selling hottest item and get that bad boy to market, then this is something you want to read. I've used this proven technique time and time again, and brought products from concept to #1 at Walmart, the biggest retailer in the world, as well as CVS, Walgreens, Rite Aid, other food/drug mass retailers, Costco, Sam's Club. You name it, I've been there. This can be done online as well. This same technique can be used to identify a major market opportunity in front of you at the largest scale. If you're a marketer or a business owner and you want to play with the big boys of retail, this tactic and this technique will show you how to do it. And if you're an entrepreneur, a small business owner, maybe you want to do it online through Amazon, this technique will work.

So, what is this technique? It's quite simple. If you want to be #1, and compete as one of the top products or services, you first need to see what #1 is. So why create the pattern for success, and why have first mover advantage, when you can actually follow and improve upon what's already successful in the marketplace, what people have already said "Yes, I want to buy" and are buying in droves? Companies are making tens of thousands, if not millions and tens of millions of dollars doing this.

> *"If you want to be #1 and compete as one of the top products or services, you first need to see what #1 is. So why create the pattern for success, and why have first mover advantage, when you can actually follow and improve upon what's already successful in the marketplace, what people have already said 'Yes, I want to buy' and are buying in droves?"*

They're selling products that they already know people want. They've already done the hard work and all you need to do is find out what these products or services are, and how much are they making. And then how much share you can take away, and how you can *improve* upon the product; how can you make your product or service even better?

Here's the proven technique I've used for years and I know works. It's quite simple: If you're playing at retail, first of all, you've got to know the category. So what category do you want to go after? Then you take a look at category data. In this case, we want to look at IRI or AC Nielsen data. This is your market research. This will determine: What is the opportunity? What is the category? How big is the market? How much share can I get? And more importantly, who is #1, #2, and #3?

"If you're at retail look at IRI or AC Nielsen data. This is your market research. This will determine: what is the opportunity? What is the category? How big is the market? How much share can I get? And more importantly, who is #1, #2, and #3?"

And that's where you need to zero in and take a look at 52-week data, 12-week, and 4-week. You can even get down to 1-week, but that's not going to tell you a lot. The 52-week will give you a snapshot of how big the overall marketplace is and an annualized volume at say, food/drug mass. You can also get that detail by retailer, broken out at Walmart or Walgreens, CVS, Rite Aid, what have you. I will say this: you can get Walmart data now through AC Nielson and IRI, but if you have FDMx (minus Walmart) you need to improvise. So my rule of thumb for you is if you get FDMx data, then if the product is listed in Walmart, typically just double the volume that you get in food/drug mass excluding Walmart. And then if that category is, say, $100 million, it's safe to almost double that and that is what Walmart's sales are. Now you have an overall view. So double it – that's the total category. Because, in my experience, Walmart's about 50% of overall sales. It's a beast, it's just a gigantic beast, and that's why people really clamor to get in there. Of course, Walmart will dictate a lot of things for you, they'll make it difficult, but that's their prerogative.

(Don't worry small business owners and entrepreneurs, I'm getting to the online component soon enough.)

So here's something very interesting. The 52-week data shows the overall category size; the 12-week starts showing you the trends. The way that they work is it's 12 weeks, year-over-year. So you can start seeing some trends and shifts in the marketplace, you see what's happening. The 52-week is year-over-year as well so you can see some minor shifts. Then you can get 4-week data year-over-year, and if possible I'd recommend getting data that's trending over 4-week or 12-week increments. So 12-weeks, maybe it's Q1, then Q2, then Q3, then you can start seeing trends in the marketplace. You'll identify who's putting their products on sale. Look at average selling price. Are they getting their volume by discounting the brand? By the way, half of product sales in the U.S. and Canada are done on sale. So that's a way to build volume. All marketers know that – if you didn't, now you do too!

> **"By the way, half the product sales in the U.S. and Canada are done on sale. So that's the way to build volume."**

The 4-week data shows you trends, and that's going to be most volatile, but it will show you the most recent trend, because you definitely want to know that you're on-trend with the product, especially if you're targeting #1.

So, that gives you your blueprint. You look at that data and say "Ok, who's #1?" Say for example that you're looking at dog food. In the dog food category, pet supplies, you look and say "Who's #1 in dog food?" and you zero in on that brand. Let's just say it's Purina. Purina's #1 brand or product is actually a grain-free high-end product that retails for $50. If you're a producer of dog food, you can take a look at that data and go "Ok, well grain-free is hot. This is the price." Take a look at their ingredient list. Take a look at their label. Start dissecting them and go "Wait a minute, I bet I can one-up that. What if I did grain-free plus probiotics?" So now the goal is to deconstruct the product and see how you can provide more value to the consumer and provide an ingredient or another attribute of the product that's very on-trend. Probiotics is on trend, so that would be an example of one. A lot of consumers want to care for the dog, want to make sure that the gut health is there. That's a good thing to focus on.

So now you bring that market, and you bring it to market with a little sales promo perhaps, or what have you. When you pitch it to the retailer, they just say "Oh, yeah this sells really well." It's less risk to them. People want the guaranteed sale, so the buyer is very interested. You know you have a high degree of confidence that this is going to sell because it's one-upping; it's an improvement of the market leader.

Buyers and marketers want the sure thing. By one-upping a #1 product you're very close to providing a sure bet to win and everyone likes to avoid failure – whether you're a buyer, the manufacturer, or the owner.

Now the next thing to do is take a look at the media spent. You can look at Kantar and other sources of media for large brands. You can start going through the list of the top sellers through IRI or AC Nielson data, then you pull your media spend data and start doing a correlation between media spend and sales. My experience has been about 20-25% of measured media is what people are spending to get the #1 slot. So this is the $y=mx+b$ equation; it's quite a linear equation. I've been testing this for years and looking at it, and that's what it is. So you have to keep that in mind; however, sometimes what you'll see is that there's a phenomenon in the marketplace where the product's just selling like hotcakes, and these brands aren't spending a lot of money. And so those are golden opportunities for you.

"Pull competitive media spends through Kantar and other sources of media for large brands… My experience has been about 20-25% of measured media is what people are spending as a percentage of sales to get the #1 slot."

Keep in mind too that you can offset growth with in-store discounting or media spend. Or both. You have to really manage that effectively. If you're going to do both effectively – you know when you're spending heavy on media and then you have an in-store program going on – I always suggest you ramp up your media before your in-store programming, your discounting, or temporary price reduction. Drop your media down, your dollars down before, just as your TPR (Temporary Price Reduction) hits. That way you can maintain the margin, you're not losing the margin. Because typically what you're going to be doing is increasing sales 30 to 100% in-store with that in-store promo – why erode the margin? Try to be margin-neutral as much as you can. It's all about profitability.

I don't want to get too much into details, but that's how you identify the #1. Identify the #1; don't go recreating the pattern for success. Find that #1 product in your IRI or AC Nielson data. Make your product or service better. In this case it's a product – make that better, one-up them. And then bring it to market. You don't need to do fancy market research, focus groups, all that kind of stuff. Save your money. You already have the pattern for success. You already know what people want. So the big marketers out there, the ones that are working with retail, that's what you need to do. And if you're not doing that already, you've just got to. Because this is a huge opportunity for you to bring brands to the top.

"You don't need to do fancy market research, focus groups, all that kind of stuff. Save your money. You already have the pattern for success. You already know what people want."

I've done this many times. I've brought brands from nothing to $15 million in under a year, or from nothing to $25, $30 million in six months. The last several years I added over $150 million combined in a year on two big national brands as part of a comeback. It's incredible, the opportunities in front of you are there... just grab them!

Now, the wily entrepreneur or wantrepreneur, the netreprenur, the small business owner, the guys looking to sell some stuff online, it's a different story. "I can't go and compete at the big retailers. I'm a small guy in comparison. That's tens of millions of dollars. I'm looking at thousands, tens of thousands, hundreds of thousands, *potentially* millions of dollars. How do I identify #1?" Well there are a couple ways. In your category, you have to look at search volume.

> *"If you're small, how do you identify #1? You have to look at search volume. There's always going to be a correlation to overall consumer demand and sales!"*

There's always going to be a correlation to overall consumer demand and sales. So in search volume, if you're the dog food manufacturer or reseller, you want to say "Ok, great, now I'm doing searches on dog food. I'm going to see that the #1 search is for grain-free dog food. Wow, there's a market opportunity there." So that's one way of identifying – look at the overall search volume. If it's in the hundreds of thousands, and there's not a lot of competition, then it's a great opportunity for you. If there is a lot of competition, then you've got to make sure you really carve out a little bit of a differentiator – again, that probiotic one that I mentioned earlier.

Here is another really important technique to use. We all know that Amazon is the juggernaut, right? The hundred billion dollars or whatever that number is. It's just insane how big this organization is. Well here's an opportunity. Amazon publishes the bestseller list. That bestseller list is your golden ticket to market research to identify who's #1. So go to Google, type in *Amazon bestseller*. Go there, the Amazon bestseller page lists all the categories – so, in this case, pet supplies. Go there, look at dog food. Click on dog food. It will show you from #1 to over 100 of the bestselling products. And if you already have a product on Amazon, and you see what's #1, you can cross-reference your sales to those sales. So you can get a clear estimation, you know +/-10%, of what you think their sales are. You can identify how much volume the #1 is doing.

> *"Type in Amazon best seller list for your category and that best seller list is your golden ticket to market research to identify who's #1 on Amazon."*

I've done that before with other products or other categories, and figured out that some of these products are selling $600,000 a month. *A month!* And these are like #5 sellers, #6 sellers. #1 sellers were crushing it even more, doing almost a million dollars a month, just on Amazon. So you can identify the top seller and then you have to make sure that there isn't a ton of competition. And how do you identify that? How many reviews do they have on their page of that product? Is it 2000, 3000, 4000? If so, it's going to be a little bit more difficult to compete against them; however, you still can. And you have to make sure there's enough margin in that category for you as well. So, like I said, if you're a dog food manufacturer, you're probably looking for 5-8 times markup in the sweet spot. There's where you can afford your cost for good operations. So you have to make sure you're aware of your shipping fees, your handling, call center costs, hosting, and whatnot. And then of course, your marketing spend.

> *"5-8 times markup is the sweet spot on Amazon. There is where you can afford your cost for good operations."*

But that's how you identify #1. You go to Amazon bestseller list, you go to the left-hand side, you search by category, you identify your category, identify the #1 sellers and see who they are, and their product offering, their product page, go to the website and see what they're doing. And then you can estimate their volume. You can go a step further and order the product and get it in your hand and really dissect it. That's the way to do it. And then go to market with your product and launch it. And you can even target that product with Amazon Product Ads. It's crazy what you can do. It doesn't mean you have to sell on Amazon if you don't want to. But that's how you identify #1 products selling online. And guess what, guys – there is a direct correlation of products that are on Amazon and at retail, for the most part, the #1 selling. So if your plan is to go to retail afterwards, do that Amazon one-stop shop to identify the bestseller. Configure your product and then go get it out online, get some proven sales, and then bring it to retail.

> *"There is a direct correlation of products that are on Amazon and at retail, for the most part, the #1 selling. So if your plan is to go to retail afterwards, do that Amazon one-stop shop to identify the bestseller. Configure your product and then go get it out online, get some proven sales, and then bring it to retail."*

This strategy really is a slam dunk. I've done this before numerous times. It is the fastest way for you to develop a winning product with less risk. If you want to determine the competitive media spend online, that's easy too. You go to whatrunswhere.com and pull your competitive data out. You can go to SEMRush.com and identify what people are spending on pay per click. You can go to spyfu.com and also see what they are doing on pay per click. Plus you can see what their organic search listings are, what keywords they're ranking for. All those things – you can identify the sales opportunity, you can see the product, the marketing. And then you can see exactly what they're spending and their creative execution. You can even go to SimilarWeb.com and research their traffic, how they get their traffic, and what their store conversions are. I mean, wow! That is the blueprint. Dissect them. Make your product better. If you can provide better branding, better marketing, better value proposition, whether that's a cheaper price or more attributes or something like that. That's the way you take share away and that's the way you get #1. This is the fast, fast proven way for you to make a #1 brand and product out there.

"Dissect your competitor using SEMRush, Sypfu, Whatrunswhere, SimilarWeb, Google, Amazon, Kantar, and IRI/AC Nielsen. You'll know more about them and how to beat them than anyone else!"

Now for services, it's a little bit different. Services, you can't go to Amazon to find that out. You can't look at retail data to find that out. In services, you're really going to have to look at search volume. That's going to be your primary indicator of market demand. And then you have to see who's ranking #1 for search and who's spending more on PPC (Pay per Click). That's going to be the way to do it. So look at guys that continuously spend a lot on PPC – you can use tools like SEMRush and whatrunswhere.com, those kinds of tools – and then correlate to their spends. You'll identify who keeps on spending. Those are going to be your #1 targets. Take a look at them, dissect them, and then see what you can do to make your service better.

I've given you a lot of tools and tactics to use and look at to go and develop a #1 product. I mean, this is gold here, guys. You can really go to market very quickly. Now, it is competitive. Somebody will probably do the same to you, so you'll be able to enjoy a little bit of freedom for several months, but this is really the nature of the game. Competition is fierce, you'll be in red bloody waters. This is the fast way to do it. If you're good at this, you can really differentiate yourself and if you have patent protection and intellectual property protection, then you're golden. If you have a unique way of doing something that nobody else can do, patent it and then you can enjoy that market space for some time.

If you're not sure about getting into IRI or AC Nielsen data, you're a marketer and you really want to get into retail but you can't afford the $60,000 a year subscription fee or the one-off $20,000 reports, that's okay. Why don't you reach out to me? I have an offer for you. Nothing in it for me, just hooking you up with great deals. Tweet me @darrencontardo and say, "Hook me up with AC Nielsen or IRI data." I will use my contacts to get you a significant discount for the category you need. This is my personal favor to you. And if you're working at IRI or AC Nielsen, maybe you should look at reducing your prices of these products and services because they're vital to marketers and business owners out there.

Ok, so more of this information will be available on the resources page, including what tools to use. I'd love to hear your success stories about how you did this and brought products from nothing to winners, quickly. You can be #1, you can absolutely do it. You can do it quickly. And you can make some significant dough doing it.

Contact me @darrencontardo on Twitter to share your success story.

Chapter 8

Create Your Brand Identity

f you're a marketer, entrepreneur, small business owner, this is the book for you.

Usually the things I work on a daily basis spark my thought process for a good old information session.

What I worked on one day was very interesting. Presentations, integration with worldwide programs at the Olympic level and sponsorship, packaging, integrated shipping options, co-packing and production, legal and half a dozen lawyers... And that's just *one day*. So, I'm sure that a marketer that works in a global organization faces those things. A small business owner maybe to a different degree, and entrepreneurs or "wantrepreneurs" face them as well, or dream of facing them. Some are fun, some are brutal.

What I think is very interesting is brand identity, particularly packaging. Typically brand is very, very important. If you're an entrepreneur, marketer, business owner, your brand is everything. What you stand for – your authentic self – that truly comes out in your brand. And depending on what industry you're in, it can be very difficult to communicate effectively what your positioning is due to regulatory constraints or legal constraints. There's always a way though. There's always a way to do it.

"Brand identity… what you stand for – your authentic self – that truly comes out in your brand."

One thing about brand identity – don't skimp out on good creatives. A creative individual is absolutely worth your money. So you're paying for their experience, the artist's experience. They can help interpret what your strategy is with your objectives and then communicate it through art. You know, things like the right typography, the colors to use and how they emote. For example, if you're working on a medical device or a natural product, those would be two entirely different font treatments, color schemes, hierarchy with visuals, the design architectures going to be different. So on a medical device, you might want blues, you might want to have an Arial – not a serif, but a sans serif font – you might want to have slight shades of green more than turquoise, whites, defined lines, showing a lifestyle orientation and progress, maybe some medical imagery. Don't skimp on high gloss, not matte. Those kinds of elements on a package or a printed material. And then music, probably soft and comforting yet strong and communicate efficacy and a clinical aspect. So, you know, think about that kind of stuff in your brand identity. You're serious, not too serious, but confident.

Now, alternatively on the flip side, you might have a natural product. With that natural product, you'd probably want to have some greens in there, you'd want to have some light orange. You'd want to communicate effectiveness but with softer undertones with a natural inspiration. So a little more breathing room with a little more focus on natural, soft, confident response. You're ultimately trying to do the same thing. It may not be as scientific though. The medical device is very science heavy but you still want to have that efficacy, just like a natural product. But the way you go about it with typography, the layout, the language that you use would be a bit different. For example, on a medical device and a natural product, you may want to say "Clinically proven" but the way you'd say it would be a bit different.

On a medical device, you'd say "Clinically proven … Class 2, etc." And then disclose clinical studies and where to get them. Whereas for a natural product you may want to say "Clinically proven for … [the benefit]." See what I'm saying? "Clinically proven to help you lose weight." Or "Clinically proven weight loss." Whatever it is. "Clinically proven skin enhancement." Versus a medical device which is probably going to be a little more intensive in your references of clinical studies because you have a different audience. Business to business, to pharmacists, whatever. Your audience is different.

Know your audience, communicate what's important to them and use visual design, typography, and hierarchy to create trust.

The brand identity is really important. You can spin your wheels with a bad designer – someone who doesn't get your interpretation and communication. Make sure you get the right artist. You can use 99designs. com, or in Canada .ca, to give a brief, have artists get your interpretation and then give you their concepts. And you'll have the option of choosing which one you feel is the most relevant for you. Or you can find a trusted source through agencies. Agencies will cost you a lot of money but typically they've done the work for you in saying "We have some of the best and brightest here and they're willing to do the work." So there's premium agencies to go after; really, a few of the big guys own everything. Or you can seek out the fun dynamic of boutique agencies that are really just a few guys that are up and comers but they may be a little more difficult to find. But again, I've worked with agencies, I've worked with freelancers, independent individuals who do a little work on the side, and then people that I work shoulder by shoulder with every day.

I've worked with some good people, and I've worked with people that have some skill gaps. And wow, does it ever show up in your collateral. So, don't skimp. Put the effort in. Find the right people. It is absolutely worth it because it's *your brand.* It's everything. And that brand reflects who you are, who the organization is, and everything you stand for.

> *"Designers... don't skimp. Put in the effort. Find the right people. It's absolutely worth it because it's your brand. It's everything!"*

One thing I would say is that identity is one thing from a design perspective but it's another thing from a personality and a corporate perspective. Make sure that you ooze your identity. You ooze what this organization is about, this DNA, if you will, throughout the organization. So if you're a small, one-stop one-guy operation, that's easy. Your brand is you. It's your personal brand. It needs to reflect that. If you're a smaller organization, say, under 10 people, it's still fairly easy but make the effort. You can get really caught up in just doing the work. Stop. Celebrate successes. Communicate to your staff, market internally, what this business is about. Why you're doing it. Who the customer is. Why you're different. And really try to be authentic and transparent with your staff and your customers; try to make sure your brand stands out.

Think of Toms shoes. Toms is a great example of this. They're all about giving back. One pair of Toms bought, one pair goes to someone in need. That is their mission, they do everything around that, and they make it very transparent. Just like Zappos and their element of customer service. Their customer service oozes as an organization and that's what they're known for. Make sure your brand and your organization stands out for something. From your design to the people you have and everything that you do, and your customers will love it. In fact, they'll understand you and know why you exist.

"Make sure your brand or organization stands out for something. From your design to the people you have and everything that you do, and your customers will love it."

What you're meant to serve and what your mission is, and how you're different. And that will really help you. You've got to be consistent with your branding. Consistency is one of the core elements of brand equity. Don't waiver. Don't just chase dollars. Be consistent. Understand why you're here in the first place. Stay your course; it'll always, always come back to you.

Chapter 9

Develop Marketing Creative That Sells

What's good creative, what's bad creative, how can you determine that, and how can you go about the creative process from a strategic perspective? Over my years I've managed big creative teams, actually the largest in-house creative team in Canada.

When it comes to creative it's very subjective. Everybody wants to weigh in. Everybody thinks they're a creative director, and as a result you can get sucked into making it a very democratic process. Because really what you're trying to do as a marketer is appeal to a lot of people; however, always ask yourself this very simple question: Is it on strategy?

"Everybody thinks they are a Creative Director. Always ask yourself this very simple question. Is it on strategy?"

It comes down to your business objectives, your business strategy, your communication plan, and your creative brief. And actually that's how the order should go. Whether you're a CEO, small business owner, or a medium size organization a few things need to happen before you even get into creative – let's just say you're medium size and have a CEO, a CMO or VP marketing or something like that. So the CEO needs to clarify business objectives with the team and if he or she doesn't do that your job becomes very difficult in establishing the creative direction, because it always comes back to the strategy. So, the framework should be: what is your business objective, what is your business plan (what are you trying to achieve), what is your strategy and how are you going to achieve that?

> *It's very difficult to establish the creative direction until the business strategy is set by yourself or leadership.*

Say you're a bank and you want to increase RRSP or 401k contributions by 5% within a certain time segment. It ties back to your objective because your objective needs to be measureable: what are you going to achieve by what date? The strategy is, how are you going to achieve it? And then the tactical stuff is, what exactly are you going to do to achieve that? My experience is people just drive straight down to the tactical stuff. And that's where creative comes in.

You have your business plan, your marketing plan, then you can have your communication plan, which includes the key messages and channels plus different messaging throughout the sales funnel – whether it's top of the funnel, which is mass awareness, down to the bottom of the funnel, which is very close to purchase. Now the creative brief itself follows your communication plan. And the creative brief really outlines: What is your objective, who is your audience, what do they believe, what's the one thing you need to communicate well, what are your mandatory elements in the brief (tagline, claims and their priority, other elements like a doctor or expert supporting your product, maybe some testimonials, maybe some legal ease you have to include)? So you'll have a master brief for your brand and then you get into briefs for packaging, TV spots, print ads, etc.

> *"Your creative brief outlines your objective, your audience, what they believe, the one thing you want to communicate, and mandatory elements in your creative."*

Hopefully you've done your research on who you're targeting, which relates back to your strategy and business objectives. And there are multiple ways to get at that. You can do secondary research, focus groups, etc., to find that consumer insight. For example, if you look at a drink. Let's say Ribena. Ribena is a drink out of the UK that is a fruit beverage – black currant I believe – and through research it was found that people use Ribena drinks not because they taste great, not because they're scientifically advanced, but because it makes them feel like a child again and comfortable, because that's what their parents used. That's what their mothers used. You have to understand that insight and then use it in your creative.

When it comes back to your creative strategy and you're looking at packaging, for example. Say you want to appeal to a male and female audience, very mass market, 18-54 and you have to do packaging. So you may want to put a male and female on that packaging or imagery that appeals to them, with claims that are mass market friendly with the insight of course that the product delivers on its intended use. Plus with the insight you have to deliver the benefit that the customer wants. So, to go back to Ribena for example, the customer wants to feel nurtured and comforted and safe so you might say "Just like mom used to make." Or "Nutrition for moms."

"Use your research, whether secondary or primary to deliver your consumer insight that will help make your creative great."

Now, if you met with your CEO and sales force, what have you, they may say "I like this image, I like that image. I like this claim, I like that claim." Every body's going to weigh in. Everybody is going to want their stake on that package. Ultimately, you have to play the political game and take their insight. However, here's how you navigate it. Turn to them and say "That's a great comment… Is it on strategy?" Then you look at the creative brief, your marketing strategy, and your business objectives. And if their comments are not on strategy, it's a pretty black and white way to tell them basically, they're off, and that you need to focus on your strategy. You'd have a man and a woman on that package, the relevant claims about how the product makes them feel, you'd drive that insight back to "Yeah, this is just like when you were a kid."

That's an important thing to know. And the key to really zero in on your target audience and make it very clear to people is by remembering this: most people don't think in an abstract way so you have to make things very tangible for them. Develop personas for your target audiences, your secondary or tertiary audiences. Give them names, personalities. So, maybe you primary target audience is moms and your secondary is Gen X males.

Everybody will want to weigh in on creative. Refer to your strategy to maintain focus. Develop personas to deliver the right message to the right person who matters – your customer.

You'd have the mom, maybe her name is Jill – a recent mom, 32 years old, with an 18 month old baby, works part time, brings the kid to daycare, has a mortgage, been married for 5 years, has a car, etc. And then the male: married, one kid maybe two, similar background. Give him a name and let's say it's Joe. And you have a picture of them. So when you talk about creative, it's easier to identify if it's on strategy. This is our target audience, this is what's important to them. Are we delivering against that?

On your creative – packaging for instance – make it physical and tangible. Make sure people giving their input can touch it, feel it, see it. Do mock ups. Don't talk in the abstract. Make everything tangible. Make sure you're talking to the right audience and have a picture of them there. And always come back to: are we on strategy? It's not a fail proof way to manage people and their input but it always grounds people and makes them think about strategy. Not about what's cool or "I like this color" but if it's on strategy. At the end of the day, your strategy is your competitive advantage. A little bling on your packaging or some cool image someone found somewhere is not necessarily going to make or break your business. And, most importantly, you need to be consistent with your brand, your messaging, and your look and feel. Consistency is a big part of brand equity. So that's how you navigate those waters.

> *"At the end of the day your strategy is your competitive advantage... you need to be consistent with your brand, your messaging, and your look and feel."*

If you really want to know how to develop a good creative brief, there are short form briefs and long form briefs. Long form briefs are probably best to start off with because they'll force you to answer difficult questions: Who are your competitors? What makes you unique? What makes your USP (unique selling proposition) sustainable – and that's the most important thing and will ensure you're insulated from competitors. It comes back to the DNA of your brand.

BMW, for example: the ultimate driving machine. Everything BMW does relates back to that unique selling and sustainable proposition. The parts they use, the engineering, the performance measurements they put into place... Everything they do. In fact, in speaking to a fine automobile, luxury brand president the other day, who works for one of the large European brands said BMW isn't a luxury brand competitor. BMW is viewed as a sports performance brand in automotive. Think about that for a second. Lots of people view BMW as a luxury brand, a badge. But in the marketing world, it is not viewed as that but instead a sports performance brand. The marketers have stayed true to their DNA. If you're looking for a car and you want performance, agile handling, but a premium product, what are you going to choose? BMW. BMW has that niche. It's not going to be an Audi or Lexus, where it has all the lush seating, etc. No, BMW seating is going to be stiffer. The shocks are going to be stiffer. The tires are going to have better handling. The cornering, the radius, it's all designed to provide that agile sports performance. The ultimate driving machine. So think about that when you're doing your brief. Really focus on your unique selling proposition and is it sustainable? It'll force you to realize, is my USP sustainable? If it's not, competitors can come and eat your lunch.

> *"If your unique selling proposition isn't sustainable competitors can eat your lunch."*

How do you get a sustainable creative USP? Patents are a good way. If you can get a patent for your product that'll really help you make your product isolated from competitors. If you can't do a patent, do you have a manufacturing process that's hard to duplicate? Do you have any trade secrets? It's really important. If you're not sure what your USP is, there's a process you can go through to get that. Look at the book *The Blue Ocean Strategy.* First, unlike Michael Porter who has the 5 Forces model, which are very competitive. You have your regulatory forces, your legal stuff, supplier, buyer, all these forces that are very competitive in nature. However, in The Blue Ocean Strategy, it says (to paraphrase): Don't fight in the red bloody waters, fight in the blue ocean because there you don't have to fight at all. You can enjoy a new market.

> *"Don't fight in the red bloody waters, fight in the blue ocean because there you don't have to fight at all. You can enjoy a new market."*

It's basically about creating an uncontested marketplace. An example would be Cirque du Soleil. Barnum & Brothers was your typical circus with lions, tigers, clowns, popcorn. Kinda dirty, kinda cheap. Targeted at kids. Cirque du Soleil said, hey, on the supply side there are a lot of gymnasts and acrobats out there who are out of work. If a lion dies of old age at Barnum & Brothers, it's very difficult to find a new lion and lion tamer. But Cirque du Soleil said, listen, there's a huge supply of acrobats. No one's appealing to an older segment and supplying a theatrical and storyline component; we can make it premium. We can create a new marketplace for the circus and have a lot of margin. Instead of $20 I can charge $75. Not only that, we can create different stories and always innovate. So they did. They created a new market space, still a circus, but appealing to a bigger, more profitable audience and with tons and tons of acrobats lining up saying "I'll be that person." If one acrobat goes down, God forbid, there's one more waiting in his place to take that job. So the model itself is pretty smart. So, again, in The Blue Ocean Strategy, that's what that is.

To identify the USP, there's something called a value strategy canvas. It's very visual but I'll do my best to explain it here. What you do is map out on an X and Y axis all the attributes of your service and those of your competitors. Map it out and put a dot where you are. Maybe you have good value, a patent, whatever it might be. Chart yourself out vs your competitors. Maybe there are other attributes you have that your competitors don't. Draw lines and connect the dots on the canvas. What you'll find is there are certain benefits that you share with your competitors, and there are always some where there are significant gaps. Those gaps reveal your point of difference. Take a look at those gaps and see if anything is protected, isolated, or sustainable? Most often, there is something. That becomes your unique, sustainable selling proposition which then, if you can do it, can become a tagline for you. That tagline will really help reinforce your positioning. Just like BMW. If you charted this out with BMW, you'd have premium, luxury, motor specs, design, agility, sports performance. That would show a huge gap between the brands. That's how you do it.

> *"To help map out your USP use a value strategy canvas, map out the attributes of your service or product and those of your competitors."*

Let's go back to creative execution. There are different messages for different mediums, and you have to understand that. This comes back to media buying to a degree. When you are doing creative, keep in mind, there's your message (on strategy), and there's also the motivation. This is key. Having had a lot of experience in the health and fitness world, I know that if I was to buy media and ship ads in Q1, that consumer is more motivated to take action than they would be in August. It's a new year, new you, you're feeling crappy from the holidays, you want to get in shape. Your motivation is through the roof. So, as a marketer, you have to make sure that your message is on point for that. If the motivation is through the roof, that means your take rates, your conversion rates are going to be higher. Then it comes back to consumer insights. What's my message, and is it unique and sustainable? Are they motivated to take action? How do I facilitate that? And your messaging should be a little different based on the medium.

> *"When you are doing creative, keep in mind, there's your message (on strategy), and there's also the motivation. This is key."*

TV is very singular in its message. Hit 'em over the head with one consistent message that should be your USP. Print is very similar but you can go deeper but not too deep. People spend on average 3 seconds looking at a print ad so make sure you get your message across in that time. Web you can go a lot deeper and guide them towards the purchase, whether that's online or offline, you can really go through the problem, solution, testimonials, scientific evidence if there's any, a good call to action, comparison competitively, etc. For banner ads, that's singular message, high awareness top of the funnel stuff.

I also want to share with you a little insight on good creative. Say you have our Ribena example. There's analysis done by Ipsos Reid, a big market research firm in Canada, they have a database of 75,000 ads and what they've found is that in advertising banner ads response (click through) rates are higher when you show a person's face and the product in there, and of course your tagline. So, really connect with the consumer. They also found that that needs to be consistent throughout the mediums. In TV they found that there's a direct correlation to the number of scenes and the intent to buy. If you have over 25 scene cuts in a 30 second spot, purchase intent drops significantly. Keep that in mind. In a 30 second spot, I believe the magic number for scene cuts is 12-13. That's about the max you want. The reason is it's very difficult to follow too many changes. You want to tell a story to the consumer, you don't want to flip flop back and forth from different imagery; it's jarring to the consumer. They'll tune out. So, not too many scene cuts, singular message, people in the ads connecting, show your product, those are important things with creative.

"You want to tell a story to the consumer, you don't want to flip flop back and forth from different imagery; it's jarring to the consumer. They'll tune out... focus on a singular message."

We could talk about creative all day long but just remember what I've told you. Let's sum it up:

* Is it on strategy?
* Manage upwards.
* Get that consumer insight.
* Identify your USP and if it's sustainable.
* Work that creative execution in TV, print, and banners.

And, by the way, with radio, you've got the longest shelf life in creative. You can go about 18 months with one piece of radio creative, plus it's cheap and fast to execute on. And when people drive, a part of the brain – the frontal cortex – is actually more open to receiving messages, so they stick longer. If your audience is commuter, radio may be a very good tool to use. You can do a spot for $100 and buy the media for cents on the dollar.

Chapter 10

Direct Response vs. Traditional Marketing

Do you know you can use direct response to build a brand? Whether you're a brand new business, a big business, or small business, direct response marketing can work for you. Unfortunately, brand purists and artists prefer image based advertising over direct response, but as a marketer, business owner, and entrepreneur I'd encourage you not to fall into that trap. What looks pretty with high production value, doesn't necessarily sell product. In fact, be prepared to spend a lot of money over the years to start to get a return using traditional image based advertising. Direct Response (DR) has a bad rap that really isn't really applicable because people think of cheap production with spots like the Ginsu knife, Sham-Wow, Sensa, and more. Typically, brand or image based advertising is used to help retail sales and DR is exactly that direct-to-consumer, but the reality is DR moves retail sales as well, plus done properly can make you way more money to the point where the retail sales are all gravy and not necessary for you to keep the lights on. At this point, the power shifts away from the retailer and into your hands.

"The reality is DR moves retail sales as well, plus done properly can make you way more money to the point where the retail sales are all gravy and not necessary for you to keep the lights on."

Brand advertising is about creating awareness, then hopefully, there is relevance to the brand (interest), creating desire, then ultimately inciting action. This process can take days, weeks, or even months before a prospect buys and requires multiple touchpoints (frequency) to get the conversion. You would typically use TV, billboards, radio, print, banner ads, PPC, Facebook ads, and everything in between. DR on the other hand is made to convert a prospect with the first touchpoint right then and there with a call-to-action. So let's use our lawyer example again – this time we'll call it "Harry's" law firm. If Harry were to take out a billboard with traditional branding in mind, it may say "Harry's Law Firm, The Divorce Experts". Or something that's brand centric and clearly communicates a position. Using DR Harry could take out that same ad, but call up the media company and say, "Hey, if you don't sell your ad unit give me a call and I'll pay 30% of the rate card," then when they call his ad creative would change to have a call to action that he can measure and convert leads to sales. It could read something like "Get a FREE 21 Step Divorce Checklist and Consultation Today at HarryDivorceFREE.com – The Divorce Law Expert, 1-888-555-5555" or "Call Harry at 1-888-555-5555. You Win Your Case or Your Money Back." The difference between the two options is that they are image based versus the direct response billboard. What do you think will get more meaningful results for Harry?

"Brand advertising can take days, weeks, or even months before a prospect buys... DR on the other hand is made to convert a prospect with the first touchpoint right then and there using a call-to-action."

This is where people get into the fundamental debate if marketing or that piece of marketing actually works because if you're using traditional brand advertising you just don't know, which is why the famous quote from David Olgivy is "50% of advertising is useless, we just don't know which 50%". Wouldn't you rather have accountability with your advertising? Well, your new Harry billboard with the 1-888# will give you just that and that's fundamentally why they call it "Direct Response;" you get a direct action from the ad and can ultimately measure its productivity for you and it should pay for itself. If it doesn't, then STOP doing it!

By now you can see the power of direct response advertising and why you don't need a focus group, why you don't need do hire a big agency, why you don't need to spend money on all image based ads like a drunken sailor. In fact, I think that advertising has lost its way in many cases. Headlines should interest your prospect and tell them clearly what benefit they'll get, long-form ad copy works better than cute, short, puns that have double meanings, and it comes down to a point where advertisers are actually scared to ask for a sale. Heck, that's why you do advertising – to sell more product!

> *"Advertisers are actually scared to ask for a sale. Heck, that's why you do advertising – to sell more product!"*

Yet another powerful reason to use direct response advertising is to forego the expensive focus groups and go right to market with test ads targeted at different segments using Facebook or Google Adwords. Why spend thousands, tens of thousands, if not hundreds of thousands on "testing" before launch vs. using ad dollars to build a pre-launch while getting your real-world consumer feedback on your brand where consumers vote with their wallet. To tell you the truth I've had to learn the hard way and have actually done both. Around 2010 I led the launch of a celebrity-based nutritional line of products and the company spent over $100,000 on the pre-market testing, this included DBI reports (this shows you how popular celebrities are), packaging testing, focus groups, media testing, regression analysis, and of course ran it across multiple buyers, experts, etc. The launch ended up being the most democratic and group think launch I've ever done. Remember, this is an image based brand launch. The results all showed that this was going to be a hit, so the launch continued and millions were spent on TV, print, web, social, and PR. The distribution was national across Walmart, CVS, Walgreens, Target, GNC, and most other FDM accounts totaling more than 20,000 retail locations. The result was a colossal failure!

"Why spend thousands, tens of thousands, if not hundreds of thousands on "testing" before launch vs using ad dollars to build a pre-launch while getting your real-world consumer feedback on your brand where consumers vote with their wallet?!"

The product wasn't selling at all and no one could figure out why, so what did I do? Worked with a DRTV producer, reshot the commercial with an offer and had the celebrity re-record the spot to test their appeal. It was a split test where one spot had the celebrity and one didn't, then the spots ran on alternate weeks in the same market to remove the variables of geography and audience and spent less than a full week of national TV. The result? The ad without the celebrity performed significantly better than the ad with the celebrity. So the products themselves were great, but we just couldn't use our celebrity who had their face and name actually on the product! It's not hard to guess what happened next? The celebrity deal was ended, they were paid out early, media cut, and the product was marked down to minimize returns while a gap fill was worked on to replace the spots on shelf. This all could have been avoided by running a test spot first in either Facebook or like I did with

TV beforehand. Don't make the same mistake and please, please, please avoid trying to appease everyone with an opinion on your team, family, or organization who frankly don't know what you do. Test small first on DR, and then go to market. You'll save money and when you have a hit will be a rock star!

> *"The ad without the celebrity performed significantly better than the ad with the celebrity. So the products themselves were great, but we just couldn't use our celebrity who had their face and name actually on the product! Test small first on DR, and then go to market."*

Testing with DR is great and a real nice advantage, but the real reason to pursue direct response advertising is to profitably grow your business. With DR you need to be cash positive nearly all the time, or at least within a period of time before your cash dries up. In DR the standard metric to watch is MER or media efficiency ratio, which is basically the same as ROAS, or return on ad spend; the measure of sales/media spend. The higher the number, the more profitable you are! You need to be above a 1:1 ratio to be in the positive of course. Imagine for a second that every ad that you put out you make money on? Would you want to spend more and advertise? Exactly, and that's why the largest brands out there that are multi-million dollar brands buying DR spots like Nutrisystem, ProActiv, JennyCraig, and the like. The benefit to being in DR is that advertising is also cheaper than traditional "premium" advertising, so your chance of increasing your profit line is higher.

> *"Imagine for a second that every ad that you put out you make money on? Would you want to spend more and advertise? Exactly, and that's why the largest brands out there that are multi-million dollar brands are buying DR spots."*

One brand in particular that did a great job on direct response and then went to retail is Sensa. Sensa was a weight-loss crystal used like salt that changed the odor of your food, so you would eat less. They started out with a long-form 30-minute commercial that told their story, the science, the testimonials, the coverage by media, etc and starting making money with their ads. Soon after, they switched to 2 minute spots that are cheaper, then to 1 minute spots, and finally decided to go to retail. They went first to GNC and won vendor of the year, then went to Coscto where they had great success, then ShopNBC, and The Shopping Channel in Canada. All of this happened within roughly a 2-3 year period where they grossed more than an estimated $200 million in sales. Unfortunately, they faced FTC challenges and ended up receding from the market due to legal challenges. However, what is incredibly powerful is how fast they grew and the immediate success they had at Walmart. Why? Because they knew the power of direct response and knew that impressions are still impressions so going to retail when you're on TV, web, and print talking about your brand even with a direct response offer would result in retail sales. Until this day it's very rare for a brand to go from nothing to hundreds of millions in sales that fast, but notables are the Shake Weightâ, Sham-Wowâ, Ginsuâ Knives, and more – so if DR works it can happen!

Imagine spending 30-40% less on advertising and still be in the same magazines, TV channels, billboards, PPC Ads, etc. as all the other big brands, but every time you do it you pay less. You can with DR. In fact, media companies have DR divisions where you can buy your ads at a fraction of the price of regular ads, so look into it and if you're not sure how to execute, please contact me at darrencontardo.net or on Twitter @darrencontardo.

"Imagine spending 30-40% less on advertising and still be in the same magazines, TV channels, billboards, PPC Ads, etc. as all the other big brands, but every time you do it you pay less? You can with DR."

Now do you think direct response is cool? Most of those who don't and prefer the prestige or look of typical brand image advertising would trade cool for profit. You know what's cool? Making money with your advertising! That's better than any special industry ad award any day! If you're a small business owner or a large agency you can do this and make money at it. Leave the brand building advertising to those big brands who can spend tens of millions of dollars in advertising over several years before they start seeing a profit.

> *"You know what's cool? Making money with your advertising! That's better than any special industry ad award any day!"*

Before I finish off with direct response I want to point out that to make yourself more profitable, you should try experimenting with up-sells and continuity programs to drive up your average order amount and lifetime value. The higher the LTV the more money you'll make and the more ammo you'll have to grow. Now go and start testing, save your money, make more money, and scale to large growth by having a top-notch sales funnel.

Chapter 11

SEM vs. SEO

Often confused and misused terms are *search engine optimization* and *search engine marketing.* Search engine marketing (SEM) is different than search engine optimization (SEO) because search engine marketing is what you pay for – Google Adwords, Yahoo, Bing! Whereas search engine optimization is the organic listing you'd find using keywords in an engine. Let's focus first on SEO.

SEO is what you use to optimize your website and web properties to show up for organic search results. If you make compression socks and someone's typing "compression socks" in Google, you want your website to show up in the white, main column of the Google results. The paid listings are above it and below – these are pay per click (PPC) or SEM keywords.

As a percentage, roughly 80% of people click on organic listings and 20% click on paid listings. Usually the best value when buying keywords is usually the third keyword – we'll go into this a bit later. For organic listings, you want to be #1. That's the Holy Grail. You really want to be within the top 3 if you can't snag the first spot. If you're not on the first page, you're probably not going to get many clicks. The reason being that about 90% of people only go through the first page of Google results before they just start a new search. So if you're on the second page or third page of organic Google listings – and I'm referencing Google right now mostly because they get the large majority of all search volume – you're not going to get many eyes.

"You really want to be within the top 3 listings if you can't snag the first spot. If you're not on the first page, you're probably not going to get many clicks."

Trust me, you want to be on the first page. So here's how you do that: Optimize for keywords. Select a handful of keywords and organize your website accordingly. If you're making compression socks, your primary keyword will be "compression socks." This probably has the most search volume; to find this out, go to wordtracker.com and sign up for a free trial to do some keyword research. There you'll find out the local and global volume of your keywords, how many websites also have that keyword you're competing for, and the likelihood that you'll rank well for that keyword. From there, you can actually build your website architecture from within wordtracker.com. I'm not affiliated with this site but it's a great service and is very effective.

Now that you've determined your primary keyword, you know that on your main page, your title tag, your H1 tag, any images, any videos you want to have the first keyword be "compression socks." Your keyword density should be about 4-5x. That means you should be mentioning compression socks about 4 or 5 times on that home page alone. Maybe another keyword you're going after is "designer." So you'd have "designer compression socks" as your secondary keyword phrase. This would be on your homepage as well as "compression socks." And if I was to click on one of these, that would bring me to another web page that shows the designer compression socks. From there you could have some more keywords. "Cheap compression socks," maybe "comfortable designer compression socks." Whatever the keywords may be that are relevant to your business. Another secondary keyword could be "CrossFit compression socks," or "Golfing compression socks," and of course you'd have related pages with relevant content.

> *"Set up your website first around the niche keyword you want to be the authority on, then make that your primary keyword and have variations of it for each secondary keyword."*

Ideally, you want one keyword as your main focus and then about 4 secondary keywords. So imagine 4 webpages that branch off of that main page. And then you'll want to have up to 4 more keywords that branch off of those secondary pages. So now you're looking at about 16-20 pages of content right there. That's how you'd build your website to link appropriately and be a category leader for your area of specialization.

The game has changed slightly now where the focus is on longer tail keywords; there are short tail keywords and long tail keywords. Short tail would be, to use our previous example, "compression socks." Long tail would be "cheap designer compression socks for women." With long tail keywords, the volume of people searching is less but it's very targeted. Imagine we are dogs; dogs love bones and will do anything to get a bone. The stronger the scent, the more aggressive we get. What we do as consumers is we go into our search engine, type in our keyword (compression socks), and if we don't see a relevant result, we will start over and go longer tail (designer compression socks for women). The first result that's closest, we're all over it. If someone clicks on your site and your content isn't what they're looking for, they'll leave immediately. That's why you see high bounce rates or bad conversion rates. If content is king, context is queen. It's the perfect marriage. That's what search engines are looking for: highly contextual, relevant information. You're the thought leader for your business. So how do you do that?

"If content is king, context is queen. It's the perfect marriage. That's what search engines are looking for: highly contextual, relevant information."

Google loves images. So tag your images appropriately with keywords. Use images and videos that are relevant; put those videos on YouTube and then embed them on your website with the right keywords. YouTube is the second largest search engine, but we'll get into that in another chapter. Get a Google+ page and mention your posts and link back to your site; Google+ actually does help your search rankings. The folks at Google don't come out and say this outright but my experience has been, yes, that's exactly what they're doing. They want search to be extremely contextual, conversational, long tail keywords, very relevant. The results are going to be about that. What conversations are you having on Google+? They'll drive back to your website.

Another thing on that: If you're the originator of your content, or you have an ebook or anything like that, sign up for Google Authorship. Why? Any search result on Google will show your picture. You may have seen this before. Guess what, people will click on that 3x more than other search results… and it's FREE. So by all means, look into Google Authorship, even if you have to publish some original content to get it. It'll be worth your business.

"List on all Google properties to maximize your search engine rankings within Google. They don't come out and admit it, but in my experience you're rankings will improve."

Back to website architecture and some things to do. The website needs to be fast; go to Google web master tools and do an analysis on your page optimization for speed. Just type your URL and run submit. Make sure your load times are very fast; if you have a site like WordPress with a lot of database calls – maybe a membership plug in, a store plug in, social media widgets – it slows your website down. I know firsthand. I did this and it killed my website. I had to blow it up and do it all over again. It's extremely frustrating and costly. If your site's mainly a store, I'd recommend going with a Shopify, Bigcommerce, Volusion, Magento Go… Something that's designed for merchandising and is already hosted and has a lot of built-in email marketing and search tools. That's in your best interest. You can use WordPress or other blog platforms and use plug ins to make a store, but it's really not ideal.

The on-page optimization is critical; we've talked about images, videos, about organizing content on there using keywords. One big thing we're missing is links. Here's a great way to get inbound links. Go out and contribute content to Wikipedia and have those link back to your website. The more authoritative those sources are, the better your site will be ranked. If you're the expert contributor on compression socks, go to forums or sites with thought leadership on that and write articles, post comments and have those link back to your site. Contribute as much as possible. Another great thing to do is start an affiliate program. This is called paid for performance marketing, where you can actually only pay out when you have a converting sale. You basically give banner ads and other like material to an affiliate who will put that on their website and link back to yours for the consumer to buy the product. If the conversion is there, the sale can happen, and that's when you pay out a cost per sale to the affiliate.

"Contribute content on big sites like Wikipedia and have those link back to your website. The more authoritative the sources are, the better your site will be ranked."

You could potentially have dozens, hundreds, even thousands of affiliate marketer publishers with advertising for your product and brand linking back to your site. That will help not only with sales but your linking strategy. Additionally, follow people on social media and try to mention them in your posts and tweets and provide links back to your site to drive traffic. Original content and curated content with tools like Shareist or Scoop.it will help you tremendously. Create content like crazy, get engaged and link back to your site, and your search results will happen. That's SEO.

Search engine marketing, SEM, on the other hand is different. You can do this really quickly; it's not as painstaking as optimization but it costs a lot of money. It's essentially an auction in a way. You're bidding to have the best placement. The more competitive a keyword is, the higher the cost per click, and this means a higher cost per acquisition. If your short tail keyword is "compression socks" and say you have 100,000 global searches for that a month but there's also a lot of competition and that keyword costs you $2 to get a #1 ranking spot, you're going to have to really pay attention to where you want to be with that. If it's $2, you have to look at your conversion rate on your website. You have to drive that keyword to a landing page with a great offer to help convert a consumer. The catch is, your conversion rate with dictate your cost per acquisition.

> *"SEM is not as painstaking as optimization but it costs a lot of money. The more competitive the keyword is, the higher the cost per click, and this means a higher cost per acquisition."*

If your cost per click is $2 and your conversion rate on your website is 1%, and you have an average order amount of $100, that won't make sense for you because there isn't enough margin in your product to actually have a cost per acquisition of $200. I've developed my own template to figure out my profit margin that you can get at themarketerscommute.com/cpcroi. With this cost per acquisition calculator, you should be able to figure out your metrics. As long as you have profit built in there, you can do this all day long. The better your conversion rate is, the lower your cost per acquisition, the higher the margin in your product, the higher you can pay. Once you figure this metric out, the better you can figure out your spend. Then you can set it in automatic in Google or Facebook. Those are great tools.

This brings me to another thing I want to mention for ads, and it's untapped: Facebook. Facebook ads from a PPC perspective are very targeted. So is Amazon. There was a study done and Reuters published an article about it: Amazon gets 50% of all product search volume online. Google gets 13%. So as much time as we spend on Google optimization, you also really need to focus on Amazon. Set up your product on Amazon through an Amazon product ads (AMS – Amazon Media Services) and that cost per click is really cheap comparatively; it goes by category. It can be as cheap as $0.20. I highly recommend you do this. It's untapped and it's not as competitive.

> *"As much time as you spend on Google optimization, you also really need to focus on Amazon. Set up your product on Amazon through AMS and that cost per click is really cheap comparatively."*

People are really looking to buy product on Amazon. Look it up! Set up your ad and your page, optimized for search just like we talked about, and you'll have probably the best conversion there as well as the cheapest cost per acquisition because people are very motivated. On Facebook you can get very targeted and go after your audience with psychographic information or whatever group they're involved in. You can do ads and point them back to your landing page or Facebook page – ideally a landing page. Even use retargeting. So if someone goes to your Facebook page and then leaves, you can serve up an ad to them that leads them back to your website. Retargeting ads is multiple times more effective than hitting up a new consumer with your ad. The reason is because when people see your ad more often, the more likely they are to convert. Look at Facebook retargeting on a PPC model. AdRoll.com is the service to use there, you can get a 14-day free trial. Again, I'm not an affiliate it's just the right thing to do. Test it out. Targeting works.

There's one more thing about SEM. If you want to do a comparison on what your competitors are spending on PPC, go to spyfu.com and you can run a competitive report on actual spends for PPC. Very effective for identifying what your competitors are spending and what volume they're getting out of it.

Stay focused, stay hungry, have an open mind. And make sure you don't overspend. Fire bullets before you fire cannon balls. Test keywords and landing pages on a small budget before you double down. Be methodical, be smart, and don't be afraid to experiment.

Chapter 12

Social Media Marketing

The golden goose: social media strategies and tactics. I'm going to draw upon my own experiences as well as what I've seen in the industry through experts and colleagues. What works, what hasn't, and some challenges.

If you're interested in this, you're a marketer, a small business owner, an entrepreneur, or wantrepreneur. We as marketers are always trying to stay cutting edge; a big part of that today is social media. There's definitely been a transition from mass media to the fragmented new media. YouTube, for instance, is the second largest search engine and can be used for your business, if it fits your type of business. Facebook – there are so many people on Facebook. Almost a quarter of the world's population is on Facebook. It really is incredible. Twitter is struggling, but still valuable for the right audience. Vine, Instagram, Snapchat, Vimeo, Google+, Pinterest, the list goes on for tools and apps you can participate in. The question is, what's right for your business and do you need it?

The one people use most often is Facebook. But how does Facebook work and how do you use it effectively? There are a lot of things you can do. The first thing you have to ask yourself is why you need it. Do you actually have to be on there for your particular business? What's your objective? What's your strategy? Are you trying to get leads? Is it a customer retention tool to foster a relationship? Are you trying to provide a value added service? What is it you're trying to accomplish?

"Facebook… The first thing you have to ask yourself is why you need it. Do you actually have to be on there for your particular business?"

Another cool platform today is iTunes for podcasting. Which, in itself, is a social tool. But I think the first thing to consider is your objective and your strategy. Most importantly, how do you view your business? Social is never ending. It takes resources. It's a real hustle play. You don't set it and forget it; it's not like paid media (see *SEO vs. SEM*). You have to roll up your sleeves, work it, be quick to respond, manage how you represent your brand, manage your communication, foster the community. And maybe the biggest thing: view yourself as a publisher. This is maybe the biggest fundamental understanding that's required. It's called social media: view yourself as a media organization, as a publisher. If you're creating a magazine, you need to create and curate your own content and then publish it to your followers. Or somehow get in the news. So let's go over some very tactical stuff.

"Social is never ending… it's a real hustle play… you have to roll up your sleeves, work it, be quick to respond, manage your brand, foster the community. View yourself as a publisher."

Okay, so let's say I think I need to be on Facebook, Twitter, Instagram, Pinterest, Google+, LinkedIn. I have a business to business component, which is important for LinkedIn, I have a consumer facing aspect so I want to get a conversation going on Twitter. Maybe I have some celebrities, athletes, influencers on my product – Twitter's a great opportunity for that. Facebook… Everyone's on it. I'm on it. So why wouldn't I use that? Google is great for search. Pinterest is visual, so is Instagram.

Okay, lots to consider. Let's first look at your niche. What is it? Say for example you're making beer. You want to be able to show the story of how it's made, the process, who the people are who make it. Open up some transparency, show your culture. Make it relevant and show social proof: people trying the beer. What were their experiences? Maybe record interviews at events, build a sense of community and increase your loyalty and following. As a publisher, you can curate content as well. There are tons of tools out there for curation. Curata is one of them, PublishThis, Scoop.it, Shareist, Storify, there's a slew of them. Say you're going to use Scoop.it. It's less than $100 a month for a business account, set it up, type in the keywords relevant to your business. "Beer making," "Beer tasting," "Best beer," breweries people follow, etc. Now you can use this as competitive tool as well. Maybe there are brewing websites you follow. There's a lot you can do.

> *"As a publisher, you can curate content as well. Curata, PublishThis, Scoop.it, Shareist, and Storify are tools that can help."*

You can point it to Google blogs, Flickr accounts, YouTube accounts. Create a story, share it, publish it to your network. So not only are you creating content, you're become a curator. Like a magazine editor, you're not only managing other writers, you're also assembling your own. You become the authority. Take the leadership role and use a tool like Scoop.it to do that. Look at all the stories in your feed, publish to your blog or social channels whatever you think is relevant to your business. It's a great way to get great content flowing. And here's a tip: The way to make that content stand out for search and relevancy – so to make sure it doesn't like you just re-pinned something – add your own comments. Scoop.it allows you to do that. Google considers that original content. So you can keep feeding the content beast and it'll benefit your search engine rankings, plus you're giving the original author credit for their content. It really is an interesting way to create fresh content. That's curation.

> *"Take the leadership role… add stories to your feed, publish to your blog or social channels… it's a great way to get content flowing…add your own comments… Google considers that original content."*

You can see how content feeds social. You have to generate content and that gives you something to share. Social, sure it's a distribution network but it's even more than that. You can look at it as *how* you distribute it as well. Even more share-ability, more engagement. If you post something and no one sees it, it's useless to you. You need original content. Ask yourself, "What are the 10 questions people are asking me today about my business?" You've got to have responses for those on your website, on your social accounts. Create videos, post them on YouTube and host them on your accounts as well. Answer those FAQs, then record 10 more videos with answers to questions you think people *should* be asking about your business. This is a system actually by Mike Koenigs with Traffic Geyser. It's a 10 by 10 by 4. Then you should create other videos with calls to action – about 4 of them – with information about where to find your product, how to contact you. Drive a call to action at the end of your other videos as well.

> *"Create 10 videos on the FAQs people ask you, 10 more they should ask you, and 4 more that have a call to action."*

I'm going to back up a little bit. Right now, people care less about words. They care more about pictures and videos. Look at your Facebook feeds, your Twitter feeds… Everything is visual. Barely anyone just types in text, and when people see just text they skip over it. We're visual beings. We want exciting pictures, shocking pictures, or videos. Keep that in mind when you're delivering your content. Even if it's just the written word you want to share through a curated post or even an original piece of content, spend the time to create an original picture, add your logo, add some type on top, make it interesting. That alone will get you multiples of click throughs, shares, engagement. That's how it works. It is a science and an art unto itself.

"We are visual beings. We want exciting pictures, shocking pictures, or videos… make it interesting."

I'll give you an example: there's a business called Shredz. Shredz is a dietary supplement. A fat loss product. It was created and marketed towards the CrossFit community. The owner didn't have a big budget but what he did was he went to these CrossFit boxes, took out a smartphone, recorded people working out, using the product, giving testimonials, and athletes at events. And then he shared it on Instagram with brand elements on his pictures and videos. That business exploded and in 10 months, he turned his venture into a multi-million dollar business. So, social can work for driving revenue. It absolutely can; you just have to be smart about it. Make sure your brand mark is on there, make sure you have engaging visuals. Spend a little more time rather than just writing some text and hitting "send." Think of it as a piece of advertising.

"Shredz didn't have a big budget… he shared it on Instagram with brand elements on his pictures and videos. That business exploded and in 10 months, he turned his venture into a multi-million dollar business."

And what I've discovered is visuals, even on Facebook, work well. Even on the ads. If you want to acquire fans on Facebook, you can create a little ad with a visual of a face or human body. People respond to that. There are a lot of studies done on people connecting with the eyes. Olay actually did this, a P&G brand; they did a lot of studies with Ipsos-Reid and found out what makes people act – find all this info in the book *Gimme! The Human Nature of Successful Marketing*, which is a database of over 75,000 ads. It's the face. The eyes, the connection. People make decisions based on emotion, even if it's a rational approach, it's an emotive response. You've done it – you've looked at someone in the eyes before and connected. That's what we're looking for. Do your ad that way.

Furthermore, for targeting and engagement drive paid likes in the advertising section. Make sure, if possible, to select the friends of friends feature. So when the ad shows up on the right-hand side or in sponsored stories, it'll say "Joe Smith," a friend of yours, "Likes BeerTown." Facebook did a study with AC Nielsen and found out that the engagement rate, the click through rate, is four times higher than a regular ad on Facebook. Four times! And a two times increase in conversion. So that one tactic – friends of friends – dramatically increases the efficiency of your spend by 400%. 200% increase in conversion. Test these things out for yourself. Start out small. Fire bullets before you fire cannonballs like Jim Collins says in *Good to Great*. Make sure you're paying attention to details because they make all the difference. Great visuals, human connection, the friends of friends feature.

> *"Select friends of friends feature in your ad… Facebook did a study with AC Nielsen and found out that the engagement rate, the click through rate, is four times higher than a regular ad on Facebook and two times the conversion."*

By the way, Facebook's head of marketing/advertising left Google to go over there. Right now Google is very expensive on a PPC (pay per click) basis. I've been doing Google Adwords for about 11 years, maybe longer, and it used to be very efficient and effective. Today, it still works, but it's very expensive. Unless you're really niche or have an incredibly high margin item, it's very hard to be profitable. If you're a direct marketer and you understand lifetime value and are willing to take a loss to acquire a customer and through up sells and cross sells and continuity programs, you can make your money back, then Google might be for you. But I will say that with Facebook, in my experience, the cost per clicks are 50-75% lower and the cost per acquisition therefore is lower. Lots of opportunity there. And it's extremely focused. You can zero in on a competitor, but it does work best with a sales funnel to drive conversions.

> *"If you're a direct marketer and you understand lifetime value and are willing to take a loss to acquire a customer and through upsells, cross-sells, and a continuity program – you can make your money back. Google might be for you."*

Example, your business, BeerTown. Maybe there's a microbrew in your area called BeerCity. On Facebook, you can actually target BeerCity fans and followers and serve them up your offer to get them on your beer. You can steal that audience, that mindshare. Very, very effective tool. Or maybe people who are following beer fests in your area – you can target them. You can't do that on Google; only by keywords.

In every instance, on every social media vehicle, your goal should be trying to get those people in all those channels on your email list. Your email list is something that you own; you own the data; you own the email addresses. And then you can use tactics like trip irrigation every time you send an email and get a little more information out of your customer. You can build information and a database. Email is still the #1 killer app. Most profitable, most effective, has the most returns for sure. People check it when they wake and then multiple times a day. They check it before they go to bed. It is a great communication vehicle. What I've found is that, typically, people are more likely to follow Facebook, Twitter, whatever, but less likely to sign up for an email. It's kind of sacred. So if you make it to their inbox, you have a very good chance of becoming profitable and developing a long term relationship with that customer.

> *"On every social media vehicle, your goal should be trying to get those people in all those channels on your email list. Your email list is something you own; you own the data, you own the email addresses."*

Twitter allows more advertising avenues today. You can do news squatting on Twitter, get in the conversation on what's trending. But make sure it's relevant. So let's say the Super Bowl is going on. People like to drink during the Super Bowl. Well, here's what we can do if Super Bowl's trending. You'll want to do a post right away using #superbowl and then the trend item is going to be about "how to enjoy beer with chili on Super Bowl Sunday." Give people something of value. You don't want to just shill your brand; you want to actually provide some value to your audience and then get into your story. Potentially millions of people can see that. If you have a call to action there that's even better. "Join our email list." "Send a text." There's tons of opportunity to get people engaged.

Chapter 13

SEM – Maximize Your Profit

Search engine marketing is the discipline of paid advertising for search. If you look at Google, when you type in a search query, in the top couple spots, usually with a color coding of yellow or pink, and on the bottom of the results, you can see paid advertising. So that's an example of marketers going in and bidding on keywords – the keywords that you've typed into the search box – with the hopes that you click on that ad and then either drive to a sale or a lead. That is, in essence, what search engine marketing is.

There are other ways to go about it – you can get into shopping feeds, you can target by demographics and interest level through Facebook, and you can also do search engine marketing through display ads and YouTube videos.

"Search – you can get into shopping feeds through display ads and YouTube videos… and you can target demographics and interest level through Facebook."

When using SEM it's important to categorize your keywords. So here's an example: If I were using high intensity training, I would have some buckets. I would have *high intensity training, high intensity interval training*, and different keywords related to that in one bucket. Then I would have misspellings of that – that would be another bucket. So a lot of people would type in *H-I* instead of *H-I-G-H* for *high*, so make sure you get that. Misspellings of *intensity*, misspellings of *training*, so you capture all of those things. Then you want to do maybe some competitive keywords. So if you know a brand that's also bidding on those keywords and is known for that, you can actually put those, that brand, into your keyword bucket. So you can have a whole competitive bucket of keywords. So if it's high intensity training, maybe you're going to be tackling Insanity, or T-25 from Beach Body.

And then there are also other terms, where it's very positive about brands, like "I love this brand. I love P90X. I love Insanity." You can put that in there. "I hate…" And then also another one is side effects: *high intensity training side effects, high intensity interval training side effects.* Those are the examples of different buckets of keywords, so you can go by the category. Again, the category would be high intensity training. And to go even further with the category and spread out the bucket of the audience, making it a wider audience, you could use *fitness training, functional training, workout, high intensity workout*, all those variations.

> **"Target misspellings, competitors, and category keywords to grow share and capture potential leads who you would have missed."**

Keep in mind that, typically, the broader the keyword, the higher the cost per click, so when you bid on keywords and you go into Google AdWords, you need to register for an account – you'll need a gmail account to do this. When you bid in your keywords, you type all your keywords in the box, and then you can estimate what the cost per click is and what position you want to be at, and the kind of volume you'll have. And then what you'll need to do is figure out what your conversion rate is on your website and what your average order amount is and then ultimately your lifetime value.

Now, it's important because eventually what you want to do is you want to turn on the automatic bidding on Google over time, so once you've identified all your key metrics, you can actually set it and forget it on Google AdWords. Then you can just base it on automatic bidding, and it'll be based on just natural conversions that you have, so you'll always be hitting your ROI.

> *"Once you've identified all your key metrics, you can actually set it and forget it on Adwords. So you'll always be hitting your ROI."*

So, with the example of a workout program, you might have a keyword bid that is very competitive and broad, it might be $2. If it's $2, and your conversion rate is 1% on your website, you've got to make sure that you're going to have an average order amount of, depending on your margins, at least $200. And then you're going to want to make sure that your lifetime value is going to be significant enough to have a return on investment. So, like I said, I'll provide a worksheet that you can use on themarketerscommute.com/cpcroi to calculate this, so you can actually calculate what your return is going to be and how much dollar margin you have. You can work on that on that sheet and manipulate the numbers.

The more narrow you go – if you said *high intensity interval training program*, which is 5 words – you would probably have less competition because there's less people bidding on that, therefore your cost per click is going to be less. And it's more targeted. When searching this, people have raised their hand and said "Yeah, I'm really interested in that" so you have a greater likelihood of a conversion rate. That would help you in your ROI. So the lower the cost per click, the better; the higher the conversion rate, the better for ROI. The higher the lifetime value, even better for ROI. So those are the key metrics you really want to focus on.

> *"The more narrow you go… less competition… so you have a greater likelihood of a higher conversion rate. That would help your ROI."*

So that is Google. Bing is also an option for you, and Bing operates very similarly to Google AdWords. You want to make sure you have the proper landing page. A landing page is critical – you want to make sure that it's highly contextual to your keyword. The best analogy I can use is what Bryan Eisenberg used in the *Call to Action* book – he said that we're like dogs. It's like somebody hid a bone on us and we're trying to get that bone. We go to Google, we go to Bing, we go to whatever search engine, and we start hunting. In this case, we're hunting for a high intensity training program that I can do at home. So you type that in, into the search box in Google and then hit submit, and you're waiting to see if somebody is going to deliver that bone to you. And then you take a look at the results and say "Ok, does it have those keywords in the title? Does it have it in the body copy? Is there a call to action for me to go get that program? Is there an offer in there?" The more contextual and relevant it is, the better. Because if you've ever done this exercise, and you search for something and you see the results and you're like "Uh, that's not really what I wanted." You're going to go back and type it a little more refined.

> *"We're like dogs. It's like somebody hid a bone on us and we're trying to get that bone. We go to Google, Bing, we go to whatever search engine, and we start hunting."*

So that's the process – we're like dogs, we're trying to get that bone. When the scent is strong, we're going for the kill. Think about that as a marketer. Make sure it's highly contextual, has the keywords, has great body copy, and the landing page has everything there. So if I'm typing in *high intensity interval training workout program from home*, when I land on that landing page, if that ad is compelling and I click on it, go to the landing page, I expect to see that copy and that whole page about that; it should be almost identical to what your ad copy was in your keywords. So that's why you want to create these buckets of keywords – one is broader, one is very specific about the category of what you're selling, negative keywords, side effects. Side effects is a great example, because that's an opportunity for you to win over somebody who might have been on the fence.

> *"Make sure your landing page is highly contextual, has the keywords, has great body copy, and the landing page has everything there."*

If they're looking like, "Ok, I'm not sure if I want to do this, what's wrong with the program, what are the side effects, can I get hurt?" You can actually have a landing page saying what you need to know about the side effects of high intensity interval training working out at home and you can convince them – well actually, there aren't any side effects. Side effects include more time to do what you love, getting more fit, all those kinds of things, not paying a gym membership, becoming more attractive, the list goes on. There's a lot you can do there. So it's an opportunity for you to really win over that customer. And if you have any studies or any social proof, put that on your landing page to convince that person who is looking for the negative to become a positive.

"Negative search is an opportunity for you to really win over the customer. And if you have any studies or social proof, put that on your landing page to convince that person who is looking for the negative to become the positive."

One thing I will mention about Google AdWords, and other tools, is that they have tools available to you to actually identify the search volume. That's quite important; that'll help you to determine budgets, what kind of volume you can expect, financial forecasts, and to determine how big the opportunity is for you. It's a great tool to do some market research. If you want to figure out if you should launch a product in this category, see if there's volume there. See if there's enough volume to build a business around, or a niche that is untapped that people are interested in that you think you can really develop. So I'll again provide links on themarketerscommute.com/resources page so you can find all the tools you need to do your proper research and identify the volume.

Alright, on to YouTube. You can actually do YouTube ads, which are owned by Google, through keywords. You can set up a TrueView ad and show your 15- or 30-second spot as a pre-roll. That is a video – it's a commercial – that gets shown to any user who is actually looking for content, video content. So again, if a user is searching for, on YouTube, *at home workout program* or *high intensity training workout program*, you can actually serve up a video with an offer to them – you have to do a 15-30 second video with a call to action on it. And so, we can set up a YouTube TrueView ad and bid on keywords just like you would on Google AdWords. And then you can set the geographic region you want to go after – Is it Canada? Is it the US? – just like you can in Google AdWords. There's a lot you can do to get very targeted. And video would be an excellent use for you because now you can demonstrate movements. It's probably even more effective than text ads or display advertising through the Google ad network. Video is very powerful. People love it. People are lazier than ever.

> *"You can set up a TrueView ad and show your 15-30 second spot as a pre-roll... that gets shown to any user who is actually looking for your content... bid on keywords just like you would on Google Adwords."*

Everybody has broadband today. People are looking at this stuff on their phones. You can overlay calls to action on your YouTube video. You can also have links to get on your Facebook, so there's a lot of things you can do there. Drive traffic to your landing page with another video that goes a bit deeper, try to convert a sale, there's tons that you can do. But use YouTube. And YouTube is actually quite cost-effective – the way you measure it is a cost per view, and then it'll show you what your conversion value is on your reporting. I've done it for direct to consumer marketing, and I've also done it just for traffic building, to drive to retail, so I'll just tell you my experience on traffic building to retail.

Traffic building to retail: On average, I get about a 10% return, meaning if I'm doing a commercial with retail tags to drive traffic to said retail, I'm actually getting 10% of people buying the product directly. Think about that – I'm subsidizing right off the top by 10% – 10% of my media spent. If you do direct buy, you should be able to get a positive return. So doing direct anywhere from 65 cents, which obviously is very positive, to multiples back. But your offer's got to be very compelling; you've got to demonstrate it like a DR (Direct Response, used in Direct to Consumer marketing) spot. It's really important.

> *"I get about 10% return if I'm doing a commercial with retail tags to drive traffic to retail... I'm actually subsidizing right off the top by 10% of my media spend!"*

With Facebook… I have to say, Facebook right now is one of the most lucrative CPC (Cost per Click) models out there, or CPM (Cost per Impression) models, because the costs are so low you can actually acquire a customer for about half the cost of Google AdWords. And ironically, the head of advertising for Facebook was the individual who set up Google AdWords. She came over and set up the whole ad network on Facebook. So think about that, the ins and outs, and how to make it even better on Facebook. Facebook you can target by competitive brand, by region, age demographic, you can target by interests, you can target friends of brands, your brands. You can go so granular in your targeting. It's not necessarily keyword related, but it is contextual enough, so you can have people who are interested in, who showed interest in high intensity training, or high intensity interval training.

"Facebook right now is one of the most lucrative CPC models out there because costs are so low you can actually acquire a customer for less than Google Adwords."

There's a lot of similarity but I find Facebook a lot more robust and there's less people on Facebook, so it's a huge opportunity for you as a marketer. Facebook is interesting, you can even drive off the Facebook ecosystem to your landing page or, get this, you can actually have your offer right in your Facebook page. There are ecommerce tools and plugins that you can use, to drive a lead – like Aweber or Mailchimp – for lead generation or to convert a sale right within the Facebook framework. People love that because they don't have to leave the platform. They can go through it, they can make a transaction, or subscribe for your newsletter or your lead, whatever that might be, your free ebook, and then you got them. You got a new customer or a new lead, all within the Facebook platform. Very, very effective – I've found that's been multiples more successful for me than driving them offsite to do a conversion because a lot of people don't want to leave their Facebook platform, so that's something to think about. And you can do ads that are sponsored stories or you can do it through the sidebar as well, which is probably the most common. There's different tactics.

"I've found driving traffic to a tab within Facebook to get a lead or conversion to multiple times more effective than offsite because people don't want to leave the Facebook platform."

Like I said, my experience on Facebook has been twice as effective and half the price of Google AdWords. The next thing I want to share with you, I think it's quite important, is shopping feeds. Google Shopping Feed is important because it's very commerce related. You just create a spreadsheet, you fill in your specs of your product, you upload it to the Google Shopping Feed, and it actually becomes part of that ecosystem, and people, when they search for your product now, will actually have results up in Google at the top, right above other search listings. So this is highly relevant for you to be able to convert that potential customer. Highly, highly effective, and you get charged on CPC there as well. I'll put that resource up on the resources page for you too so you can navigate that.

And lastly, as a bonus, I'm going to talk about something else that's really untapped. It is unbelievable: Amazon Product Ads. Highly, highly effective, very low cost per clicks – 25-45 cents depending on your category. Unchartered territories, not a lot of people are using it. Amazon has just gone after Google in such a significant way. I mentioned earlier that well over 50% of people looking for products start their search on Amazon.com. By the way, it's less than 13% on Google. Amazon knows that, so they started their own product ads, where you can actually create product ads on Amazon to drive to your Amazon store to drive the sale. I think it's a huge opportunity for a savvy marketer and entrepreneur to really drive a lot of interest for your brand and your product. And even your service. So if you have a service, you might be able to package it in a product through an ebook.

"Amazon product ads are highly effective… very low CPC… unchartered territories with not a lot of people using it."

Another thing to look at for SEM: There are some research tools that really help you analyze your competition, set up your campaigns, monitor success, do your research. You can find out what your competitors are spending actually, and what keywords they're going after, their total budget. It's really remarkable. A few of these tools:

* SEMrush.com – a fantastic tool to do this analysis.
* Spyfu.com – another great resource for you.
* whatrunswhere.com – this is a little different but still works.

Well, we talked about a lot here for search engine marketing. We can go on and on and on about little tactical things to do, but – like I said – I'm going to have a lot of resources for you on the resource section of the website. If you're good at this, you can get a really good return for every dollar you spend. I typically get a 4 to 1 return on my AdWords and other PPC campaigns – Facebook, YouTube. So think about that – for every dollar I spend, I usually get $4 back. How would that change your business? For every dollar you spend, getting $4 back. Would that be worth it? I think so.

"I typically get a 4 to 1 return on my Adwords and other PPC campaigns – Facebook, YouTube, etc. How would that change your business?"

Section 3

Advanced Digital Strategies –
That Don't Break the Bank

Chapter 14

SEM Expanded – Discover How to Use PPC to Drive Max Profit

The cousin to SEO is SEM or search engine marketing, which is the paid search advertising. If you look in the top couple spots of pay per click words in Google or Bing those are the paid ads of SEM. You can target your customer by geographic region and interest as well as the actual keyword to make it more relevant. SEM is great to exhaust first before moving on to other paid media because you get the most relevant audience who is searching for your product.

> *"SEM is great to exhaust first before moving on to other paid media because you get the most relevant audience who is searching for your product."*

You can also do SEM though display ads and YouTube videos – there you can target through keywords. If you use high intensity training as an example I'll show you how you can bucket your keywords to optimize performance. If, for example, someone types in "hi intensity training" that would be a misspelling and we would create a bucket of all variations of misspelling that could fit our category or product. Another would be competitive keywords and brands, then a bucket of love. Such as "I love high intensity training" or "I love working out". Another is the "I hate" bucket to get people who are leaving or showing displeasure with your category or product. It's a great way to save the sale and do a win-back campaign. Here are your options for keywords:

Brand
Category
Competitors
Positive "love"
Negative "hate"
Adjacent or complementary products

Keep in mind the broader the keyword the higher the cost typically because there is more competition for that term. The long-tail of keywords will get you lower cost and higher conversions, but the problem there is the volume or demand is much lower.

> **"The long-tail of keywords will get you lower cost and higher conversions."**

So how do you set this up? Go into Google Adwords and create an account. From there you can use the bidding tool to determine your budget, keywords, ranking you want and ultimately your estimated number of clicks. To bring it to the next level and close the loop on reporting you'll need to measure your conversion rate, average order value, and your life time value. Once you figure that out you'll know what you can afford to spend to acquire a customer to be profitable. If you are concerned on how to do this I have a free worksheet you can access that I created just to solve for this that you can get here: themarketerscommute.com/resources

"To bring it to the next level and close the loop on reporting you'll need to measure your conversion rate, average order value, and your life time value."

You'll need to figure this out to set up the CPA model on Google – that really is automatic bidding that helps hit your ROI on an ongoing basis and it is a set it and forget it system. The higher the margin the easier this will be for you.

Remember these simple rules for KPIs:

Low CPC
Low CPA
High CVR
High AOA
High LTV
Low Bounce Rate

Great, now what? You need landing pages to make this work! You need landing pages that are highly contextual to the search term. Bryan Eisenburg said it best in his book *Call to Action* when he said we are all dogs! Meaning that when we search using Google we are looking for our bone and the stronger the scent the more we dig. If you type in "I love high intensity training" and click on the ad, then land on a page for water aerobics you're going to leave that page in an instant, which is why your bounce rate is important to look at. If you land on a page with testimonials all about high intensity training and how people love it and how to get a program on this high intensity training for people who love it then you found your bone and will likely convert. Here are some tips on how to make your page more contextual: put the ad copy in the headline, put the ad copy in the body copy right away, have a call to action related to the ad copy, and if you can have a video related to the ad copy. That will most likely get your customer to take action.

> *"When we search using Google we are looking for our bone and the stronger the scent, the more we dig."*

Now with some more context let's circle back to an important keyword bucket; the negative keywords. This is your golden opportunity to get your customer at the point of defection, which is cheaper than winning them back or even acquiring them. Let's use the example of "high intensity training side effects". If someone types that in you should be bidding on it with an ad like:

"High Intensity Training
Side Effects You Need to Know
How to Prevent and Fix
High intensity training.com/side effects"

That brings you to your landing page with the headline:

High Intensity Training Side Effects

Everything You Need to Know About How to Prevent and Fix the Side Effects of High Intensity Training

Did you know that some of the side effects of high intensity training are due to bad nutrition? That's right if you eat a meal balanced with essential protein, veggies, and a fast absorbing simple carb after training you can delay muscle soreness and recover faster?

Not stretching prior to or after high intensity training can cause minor tendinitis, which can easily be prevented with 5 minutes of stretching.

Another benefit to high intensity training is that you can get a total body workout done in just 20 minutes versus traditional gym routines and save yourself hours of time!

Research shows you can burn more fat using HIIT than you can doing other working out.

Etc…

You can see how powerful it is to be able to use these keywords to help block a customer from leaving can be or even help build your business.

"Get your customer at the point of defection, which is cheaper than winning them back or even acquiring them."

Another great option for building your business is to use the Google keyword tool to see what type of search volume is there for your product or category prior to even entering into the space. If there are a lot of searches and a breakout of interest you may be onto something… especially if there isn't a lot of competition out there bidding on the keywords or even in the market. I have done this in the past using Google before going into a category and it is by far the most valuable measurement of true consumer demand… even better than historical sales data for competitors because it shows interest on potentially new white space ideas (niches).

"Use the Google keyword tool to see what type of search volume is there for your product or category prior to even entering into the space."

YouTube

You can actually do keyword ads through YouTube, which is the 2nd largest search engine in the world, but you will need video assets to do this. With the TruView ad module you can upload your 15 or 30 second pre-roll video into YouTube and put your keywords against it. The beauty with this strategy is that YouTube will give you a better story telling platform and you can build awareness in addition to true conversions at the same time. A trick I've used historically is that I have put annotations on the ads to click to the landing page before the spot is over and then near the end of the spot I make it look like it's done. Why? Because YouTube only charges you for a complete 100% view of the commercial. Another insight is that people are loving videos today and are lazier than ever! My experience for traffic building to retail sales have been about 10% direct subsidy, so for every dollar I spend to drive to retail that I also have a link back to the site where the customer can buy.

"A trick I've used historically is that I have put annotations on the ads to click to the landing page before the spot is over and then near the end of the spot I make it look like it's done."

Facebook

A very lucrative CPC model with lower cost than Google at this point, but you'll need an email funnel for this to work really well. Although not keyword related per se, you can hyper target your audience even better than Google. Additionally, you can add a plug in right within Facebook to let people buy within Facebook so you don't even have to go to a landing page. It's worked for me as well, but prefer the email funnel so I can up sell them on the checkout.

Shopping Feeds

Not really used that often, but if you have a store you should be putting your products into the Google Shopping feed. These get on the top listings above others on google.com and great at conversions because the customer can see the picture and price.

Amazon Product Ads Through AMS (Amazon Marketing Services)

If you're listed on Amazon you need to use Amazon Product Sponsored Ads within the Amazon Marketing Services system. Costs per click are very low and conversion is high on Amazon. You can also get a lot of tips and tricks on Amazon Media Services YouTube page.

There you have it. The SEM action list to go after and build your business. I typically get a 4:1 return on my SEM efforts and you should be profitable too if you follow these practices (provided you have enough margin in your product or service). Now go out there and get moving!

Chapter 15

SEO – Discover Free Traffic

Search engine optimization (SEO) can be very lucrative, and it's changed dramatically over the course of the last several years, and especially the last year, or even 6 months. You know there are new updates people talk about all the time – Panda update, Penguin update, Hummingbird, etc. And so if you're a techie and you're really into SEO, you know what I'm talking about.

The majority of people don't though, and that's okay. I'm going to break it down, and tell you what you need to do to really take advantage of SEO and build a good strategy. It's really not that difficult. It is a bit of hustle – there's no doubt about that – but you can be quite successful. Now, is it as effective, is it as easy as it was years ago? No, it's a lot more difficult now to get a top page ranking for your keyword, but it is possible.

> *"SEO is a bit of a hustle – there's no doubt about that – but you can be quite successful. It's a lot more difficult now to get a top page ranking for your keyword, but it is possible."*

So I want to first draw a line in the sand between search engine marketing (SEM) and search engine optimization (SEO). SEO is about on-page optimization. So the content you have on your website that's optimized for search engines that are indexing it – the Google or Bing's of the world. Those services have spiders, bots, that go and crawl your website and then send that information back to the search engines.

Typically what you want to do to help that is put a site map on your site; that'll help this bot index it more effectively. You can go onto Google webmaster tools and there's a service, an index service that you can use, that you can put on your site to help that spider index it more effectively. If you are doing it yourself, that's where you go. If you have a developer, ask him about it to make sure that they're doing that properly.

Then there are other elements of SEO, which would have inbound links and whatnot – we'll talk about that – but there are a lot of updates. It's hard to navigate, but it's quite simple.

Now, SEM is all the paid advertising, so Google AdWords, Bing Words, you can even go into the shopping sites, shopping feeds like shopping.com, even Google's marketplace. Now Google has an unfair advantage because they'll actually list results for the shopping feed in Google searches, in addition to YouTube and other services. So, with SEM, you have control of copy – you can develop your ad copy, bid on your keywords, create keyword buckets, and then drive to a landing page with an offer, lead generation, whatever it might be.

For SEO the biggest update (as of when this book was written) from Google is called Hummingbird. And basically, what that has done is it really has kind of flipped SEO upside-down. So you might have had people before who are really good at keyword stuffing. Keyword stuffing is the principle or the practice of putting one keyword on a page multiple, multiple times. They would put it in the title tag, so if you look at your search engine or your browser, it would say what that page is in the very top, in the blue bar – that would be your title tag. They put it in the title tag, they put it in the H1 tag, they'll put it in the first word or the first sentence in the body copy, they would bold it, they would put it in the body copy about a dozen times, they would have images with alt tags on it, they would have a hyperlink to it, and with other pages as well, from other pages into it. So you see where I'm going here. They stuff it.

The *proper* keyword density actually is about 4-5. You shouldn't have your keyword in there more than that. If you're using WordPress, I would highly recommend SEO Yoast as a plugin. It'll bring you through the proper ways of optimizing search for your page. It's something that I've used in the past, in addition to just hand-coding the proper keyword architecture on a page.

> *"The proper keyword density is about 4-5. I highly recommend SEO Yoast as a plugin for Wordpress. It'll bring you through the proper ways of optimizing search for your page."*

You need to have good page ranking; Larry Page developed PageRank through Google, and you can get a Google search bar put onto your browser to identify what your PageRank is. And the higher the PageRank, the better.

There are 3 elements I think that you need to look at though when you're looking at search engine optimization.

The first one is on-page optimization. We talked about that. Optimizing for the keyword you're going after. So say for example, I'm going after hair loss. I'm bald by the way, so it's relevant for me! Hair loss – I would put in my title tag, I would put *hair loss solution* maybe. In my title tag, in my H1 tag, in my body copy, have images with alt tags on it. I would have inbound links from other pages with the words *hair loss solution* built in. I would have a product sell on that page because my goal here is to have a product that has *hair loss solution* as the keyword. So here's your opportunity to use it almost like a landing page. So, on-page optimization is one. That can account for about 40% of your optimization for keywords.

*"There are 3 elements you need to look at when doing SEO;
1. On-page optimization, 2. Authorative inbound links, and
3. Newsworthy relevancy."*

Second, we have authority, authoritative inbound links. If you want to increase your PageRank and the traffic to your site, what Google wants to know is: is this site legit? Is it an actual business with a contextual answer to the query? Or is a savvy bait-and-switch SEO expert? They've done a lot of work really trying to weed out the crap and get to the legitimate sources of information. So say for example, you have your product for sale at Walmart.com. Walmart.com is going to have a huge PageRank. They're legit. Everybody knows Walmart. This is the real Walmart. If you had a link back to the manufacturer, which is you, and you had a link back from Walmart to your page, Hair Loss Solution, your authoritative ranking increases. Your PageRank increases. Google sees that, follows the link, and says "Wow, that's a reputable source going to this site. They must be the real deal."

So if you had a link from the FDA government site or a publication, say for example *Men's Health* magazine. Say you did a buy, a digital buy or some sort of product plug with *Men's Health*. Negotiate a link back to your site because they have a higher PageRank and that'll come back to you, and now all of a sudden, your authority increases. That's *link love*. Google loves that – it's inbound linking and it's authoritative. You want to get a lot of reputable inbound links to your page with that keyword to increase your PageRank and make sure it's optimized on-page.

There's a tactic that was often used years ago – not even that long ago – called link-baiting. You don't want to do that. What you want to do is build legitimate relationships with advertisers, with vendors, with anything like that to drive to your site – otherwise Google will penalize you. Another tactic you can do is go on forums – reputable forums. Maybe there's a hair loss forum where men talk about hair loss. Well you can go on there, build a rapport, have a link back to your site to this page to increase the authoritative ranking. Maybe you do a guest blog post on fastcompany.com and talk about innovative hair loss solution, and then you link back to your site.

> *"Post on forums and legitimate sites and link back to your site to increase your PageRank. Google loves it."*

Think about that. Be creative. There are a lot of things you can do on your own, or your peer company can do for you, if you have one, if you're fortunate enough to have one. Ask for love back from vendors, from your publishers. There's a lot of opportunity to increase your search engine inbound link love. So, that's probably about 30%, maybe 40% of it.

And then the third component is relevancy. News-worthy relevancy. This is where social comes in. This is very interesting now. So, for example, people are talking about hair loss in the news or celebrities are talking about it, or you have experts talking about it on Twitter, on Facebook, on Pinterest, Tumblr, anything like that. What you want to do is comment on it and link back to your site or have them have links to your site. You want to get in on the conversation there. You know, proper hashtags, and then even relate it to your article or to your page if you can. That would be the best thing. Even if you embedded that Twitter conversation and put it on your actual page, that would be great. Now all of the sudden, you have a perfect storm. You have new and noteworthy, as far as the conversation in social, so that is relevant. You have your page optimized, and you have inbound links from authoritative sources. That's really how you do it.

> *"News relevancy is social so use hashtags, links back to your website (ideally to a landing page), and even if you embedded*

a Twitter conversation on your actual page, that would be great."

I've done this – not even that well – I would say, the social component not as well as I should have, the inbound links from other sources for my wife's business – she's a personal trainer and fitness writer and has her own fitness program available online as well as her own gym. Her gym is called HIT Club Fitness and her specialty is high intensity training. So we focused on keywords *high intensity training* on her website – by applying these practices, and not perfectly whatsoever – and we were ranking on the top page in Google. And that was in 6 months. It doesn't happen immediately. It does take time. It's not like a paid search engine marketing campaign where you flip the switch and it's on and you can drive traffic right away. However, the business with hustle and the traffic with hustle is there, and it will gradually build over time.

The rule of thumb is to develop great content too. Keep your content fresh. Keep on adding content, all about hair loss, if we're using that example. So, if I want to structure your site about content – this is a key component of on-page optimization – you want to talk about your hair loss a lot. So if your hair loss product is there, your home page is going to be *hair loss solution* or *hair loss brand name*. Then you want to have secondary keywords, about 4 of them. So imagine 4 pages. That's going to be *hair loss tips and tricks, hair loss preventive measures, hair loss quick fixes*, and then *hair loss how to cope.* You'll find out through your proper research what keywords are relevant to you. So now you've created 4 pages off your homepage. Then after each one of those 4 pages, you can have another secondary set of keywords. So let's call those primary keywords and now give them another set of secondary keywords. And you can probably go another few levels deep. Relative to hair loss prevention, you might have *hair loss prevention methods, hair loss prevention tips*, and other keywords that people are searching for about prevention and hair loss.

"The rule of thumb is to develop great content. Keep your content fresh. Keep adding content around your keywords."

You can structure this in a sound way that's very visual, and relative to the amount of keywords and competitive keywords out there that people are using to optimize their pages. You can use a tool to really help you, and this is what I did. I went in to my wife's website and looked at *high intensity training*, I used Wordtracker. Wordtracker has been around for a long time, so it'll help you identify how much traffic is out there for your keyword, how many websites are optimizing their pages for those keywords, so what the relative competitive score is, and you want to find something that isn't that competitive, and doesn't have as many pages. And you can then structure your whole website through a chart of your primary keywords and secondary keywords. You can map it out and that'll be your architecture for your website: how many pages you need, what the pages are, how things flow, how to develop your content. So that's what I did with her high intensity training business.

And that's how we became #1, well top 5 actually on Google within 6 months. We developed content and, like I said, the inbound links weren't as good as they should have been and the social news and noteworthy news wasn't as good as it could have been. There's an opportunity there to rank up to #1. If you do this properly, go to Wordtracker, you do your research: What's my primary keyword I'm going after? What are my secondary keywords? How much competition is there for my keywords? Structure pages, develop your content, keep your content fresh, use a blog if you have to keep that content going because Google loves new content. The more content you have means you're going to be a reputable source of information. Have inbound links from authoritative sources, either paid or earned – some you may do yourself, some you do with publishers, some you do with vendors. And then get in there with the news. Get new, noteworthy people who are in the news talking about this stuff linking to you. Having a hashtag relative to you, to your brand, that will all work.

> *"What primary keyword are you going after? What are your secondary keywords? How much competition is there for your keyword? Structure your pages, develop your content, and keep content going to be a reputable source of information. Use Wordtracker to help."*

If you have keywords that are generating 100,000 searches a month, imagine you got 10% of that. 10%! 10,000 more visitors to your site. What can you do with that? You can change your business – whether you're a start-up or an existing organization or marketer. Now you have the tools. I gave you the WordPress example with SEO Yoast. WordTracker as your starting point to set it up. How to optimize on-page, how to get authoritative links, and then how to get into news through social media.

Key little bit of information: If you want to do an audit of your existing site, go to SEOmoz.org to run an analysis of your website to find out how many broken links you have; is it optimized for keyword. You can also use webceo.com, a tool to do that analysis for you. There are a lot of options, a lot of cool tools, a lot of great things. I will put these resources up on themarketerscommute.com/resources – go optimize your site and make some money! Get noticed. Get relevant. And get your brand out there. Now you're armed and dangerous.

Chapter 16

Develop a Winning Content Strategy

Building out a content strategy: As you know, you can do two things with your media – you can buy a lot of media, or you can develop a lot of media and become an authority. The two kind of co-exist in a unique way. At the end of the day, you need to view your organization as a media company and as a publisher. So just like a great magazine, a great television show – there's content that is published, and then they attract advertisers. That is typically their model to make money.

Now you're a bit different, right? Maybe you want to develop content to sell your own goods or services. So here is a framework that you need to think of for content strategy: you need to teach, educate, provide entertainment, and utility. Then recognize and reward your customers, prospects, fans, and loyalists. That's really how simple it is.

> *"You need to teach, educate, provide entertainment, and utility. Then recognize and reward your customers, prospects, fans, and loyalists. That's really how simple it is."*

You can spend a lot of money and get your message out there, but what I would urge you to do first is to really help solve problems through providing utility or education or value-added services; provide an experience. So when somebody buys your product or service or interacts with your organization, you give them an experience that nobody else can. I think I may have touched on this before in previous ebooks, and there's also a great book called *The Experience Economy*. The best way I can describe what an experience is is by looking at Medieval Times. Medieval Times – you probably know of – it's a medieval theatrical experience that you can enjoy with friends and family over dinner. They give you chicken and potatoes and a goblet of beer or wine, and you watch knights joust. You have the good and the bad knights and they have all these battles, if you will, like medieval times with a little bit of storyline. So the question you have to ask yourself is: Do you go to Medieval Times for the food? Or some good chicken? Or do you go there for an experience?

> *"I would urge you first to help solve problems through providing utility or education or value-added services; provide an experience. So when somebody buys your product or service or interacts with your organization, you give them an experience that nobody else can."*

Well, the product is food, but the service and the experience is that theatrical component that makes Medieval Times unique. So you leave there going "Wow, I had a great time. I sat through a two-hour, three-hour dinner. My plate was on an old rustic metal dish, my goblet looked authentic." And then they have merchandise they sell later on as part of that experience. They've kind of done for dinner theatre what Cirque du Soleil did for the circus. So a bit of a blue ocean, but more importantly, they provide an experience, just like Cirque du Soleil did. They provide an experience they can charge a premium for. So that helps them develop great content.

When you approach your own business, you have to ask yourself: How can I give my customers and prospects an amazing experience that creates a competitive advantage and insulates me? So you're insulating yourself from other competitors. Your customers won't want to go to those competitors because they don't get the same level of service.

"Ask yourself how you can offer an experience nobody else can so you can get a competitive advantage and insulate yourself from the competition, increasing sales and ultimately loyalty."

Another example are the banks. Have you ever worked with a bank and they provide great service, you know the person's name at the till, at the counter? They offer you all these services, they have great hours, they call you with follow-up, offer you ways to save money – that creates a cost of defection. That's what they call it – the cost of defection, meaning you will not go anywhere else because that service is great, the experience is great and if, frankly, it's a pain in the butt to go and transfer to somebody else, even if they might have a little bit of money saving on their checking account or their interest rate on their credit card or their points card, that's better. Your bank has created an experience and a level of service for you that you value; that's all value-added. You're not really paying for it. That value-add is so strong, that relationship is so strong, the experience is so strong, there's a cost of defection. It's not worth it for you to leave to save a couple dollars. So those are good examples of experience.

And so how you map out your content is really about:

1. How do I provide utility, or value-added services and education to my audience?

2. How do I entertain them? So how do I package it in an entertaining way that they'll want to digest it and share it and be engaged with it?
3. How do I recognize my audience? How can I put them at the forefront?
4. How do I reward their loyalty?

That framework will provide you with a lot of content that you can develop on social, through micro-content, by having a little bit of different content on Twitter, Facebook, on Pinterest, visuals, videos, appropriate dimensions. Then on your website alone, and also guest posts.

> *"The 4 question framework will provide you with a lot of content that you can develop on social, through micro-content, by having a little bit of different content on Twitter, Facebook, on Pinterest, your website, visuals, and videos."*

So now we can get into the nitty-gritty of the content. There is a 10x10x4 strategy for content development made famous by Michael Koenigs of Traffic Geyser. I recently did a post on this on LinkedIn, about ways to develop a great content strategy. This is one example. So basically, it comes down to Frequently Asked Questions. FAQs are a very powerful tool for your business and your website. The first 10 questions are the 10 questions that customers are asking you today. So go talk to your customer service center, maybe you know them because you're interacting with customers, go on Twitter – what are people talking about? Maybe you have it in an email. Go through them and discover what the 10 most common questions are.

Then develop videos in response to those questions. Post them on YouTube, post them on your website, plus have the written word. Then go and write down 10 questions that your customers should be asking you. Now these are devised to develop your niche, to really show your expertise, that your product or service is what they want. The best within your niche. You're the #1 – show them why. An example could be: why Brand X is the best choice for this audience. There are so many different examples you can use, but there are 10 questions you should develop related to exploiting your niche, exploiting your point of difference. And then those are presented in the form of videos and written word. Post them on YouTube and embed them on your website.

"Use the 10x10x4 strategy for video content based on FAQs made popular Mike Koenigs."

Then, you'll need 4 more videos. So now you have 20 videos done and now there's 4 others. One of them really is just "Go here for more content, go here for more answers." So it's just a video saying "Hey, you have a bunch of questions, we have a bunch of answers. Go here for more," which links up to all your FAQs and videos. Then there is a video that you create that basically is a lead generation. "Get all 20 videos, video series, now just subscribe to our email list, all the content you need about our business." So that's a lead. And then have another video you create on the thank you page from your lead. So say, "Thank you for subscribing and becoming a member of our mailing list and getting these videos. We hope we helped you. We're looking forward to serving you." And then just have a call to action to learn more and consider the sales. That links to a sales page. On the sales page, that's where you create another video, which is really asking for the sale. Now you say ok, you have everything you need, what makes this different, what's the problem, what's the solution, how are we unique, what's the credibility anchor, social proof and testimonials, and then boom, hit them up with your offer. Call to action – ask for the sale. And you can put that video up on your site – different spots – on your blog, at the bottom of your email newsletters. If you've proven your worth to the customer, don't be afraid to ask for money.

So that's one example – that's a 10x10x4 video example. People love video. And you automatically can dominate search engine, specifically the YouTube search engine. Don't be scared to do video. I know it gets scary; you become vulnerable. But it ultimately is worth it; just get over yourself. And if you can't do it, you really can't, you're too insecure, you hate how you look on camera – and I get it, I understand it, video is humiliating at times – have somebody else in your organization do it. Or a friend. Maybe you can hire a local actor. There's always an option for you to get somebody to do it if you're just really not ready, not comfortable creating a video, putting yourself up there. I understand. But I'd urge you just to get over yourself and do it. Rip off the Band-Aid.

"Don't be scared to do video. I know it gets scary; you become vulnerable. But it ultimately is worth it; just get over yourself."

The next thing for great content strategy is to go deeper with more questions, to really go deep. All of these questions – anytime you think of a question that relates to your business, write it down as an FAQ and that will help for search engine ranking. And link it out to other pages in your website. And if you want to get experimental you can do video with that too – the more videos, the better. That's incremental content.

Then I think the biggest component is the utility factor. So say, for example, you are selling a piece of fitness equipment. Maybe it is like the TRX. TRX is a brilliant example of content. They actually have a lot of how-to videos, and education, that make the how to use their product more effectively on their website. They really built their brand through education and on YouTube. So now it's just like, okay well how do you use my piece of equipment to lose weight, to build strength, to train like an Olympic or an elite athlete, how do you use it in a hotel room, or 101 uses for my product. And then really put your head in the mind space of the consumer. Say, "How can I get as many uses and utility out of this product as possible, so I can create value?" Then maybe you want to go a bit further and link people up into a community. And now you get user-generated content; ideas that can be shared on how they use the product together.

> *"The biggest component of a content strategy is the utility factor. Put your head in the mind space of the consumer. Say 'How can I get as many uses and utility out of this product as possible, so I can create value?'"*

Then you want to curate content. So using tools like scoop.it, shareist. com, curata.com, and storify.com can curate content. Find content out there by keyword or channel or blog or video, share it with your audience and add your own twist to it that you think will have some utility or maybe entertainment value to your consumer or your prospect. Google loves it because it's new content because, yeah you've curated that content, you've borrowed somebody else's, you're giving them links back to it, but you're also adding your own little spin to it, adding more content. You publish it on your own platform, share it across social. And now Google says "Oh, that's original content. And there are links in it. And it's relevant socially." That helps you from a content perspective.

So you've created your content, you're curating content, you're linking it up to social. Now I would ask you to reach out to your users, reach out to your fans, your avid fans and say, "Hey, who wants to become a contributor? Who wants to generate content for us?" These are like little freelancers. Imagine you have a magazine and people are contributing content, or like CNN does now where you can take a video and upload it and share it. Allow your fans and your customers to become contributors. That gives them recognition. You are giving them recognition for a job well done and being engaged in your business. That allows them to become more engaged, more engaged in social, better for search. You can see now that it becomes a perfect storm.

> *"Ask your fans to become contributors to your cause and that gets them recognition and boosts your content/SEO as well."*

And then, the last thing you can do is reward them. Reward them for actually becoming a great customer, for contributing great content, for achieving something. Maybe you want to highlight a customer that's achieved, with this fitness equipment, a weight loss or built more muscle and submitted a testimonial. And by the way, solicit for testimonial. Through email, Twitter, Facebook, whatever you want to do for your platform, reach out to them and say, "Have you had any success with our product? We'd love to hear your stories. Please submit them to…." And then you can share those pictures, those videos, those stories with your fans, your followers, and highlight somebody who's had great success. Share in their victories, relish them, make them feel like they're the most important person in the world. They're your valued customers so, really, they are.

> *"Solicit your customers for testimonials. Through email, Twitter, Facebook, whatever you want to do for your platform, reach out to them and say 'Have you had any success with our product? We'd love to hear your stories. Please submit them to…' Then you can share those pictures, videos, and stories with your fans."*

Think about it from a real-life example. You probably know people that make you feel really special. When you see them, they're excited to see you; they ask about how you're doing, they ask if there's something they can do for you. Think about your grandmother. In fact, your grandmother is a perfect example. Your grandmother is always happy to see you (I hope!). She wants to bake and cook for you. She says that she loves you. She says that she's always thinking about you. Maybe she knit something for you. It's always about you, and it's not about her. She makes you feel like you're the most important grandchild in the world, the most important, loved person in the world. Like she's taken a page out of *How to Win Friends and Influence People*. If you bring the principles of *How to Win Friends and Influence People* to your content strategy and to your prospects and fans, through social, you will kill it. You will absolutely kill it. You'll become a magnet for people, a magnet for your business. Revenues will go up because everybody wants to feel special and loved.

"Treat your customers like your grandmother would treat you!"

Think about that for a second. You can change your business by making people feel great and celebrating them, showcasing them, rewarding them, getting them engaged. It is truly remarkable what could be done. And that's a very simple thing to consider. There are a lot of tactical things we talk about all the time because, as marketers and entrepreneurs and small-business owners, we're looking for the edge. We're looking for the latest and greatest tactic out there that can help make us some money. We're looking for the roadmap for success. What better roadmap than making people feel wonderful? Make them feel like the most important person in the world. You do that personally and through your content plan and social plan, you really have a perfect storm. Who wouldn't want to do business with you?

Just keep on providing that experience, that utility, that value-added service, that great piece of entertainment. Recognize your fans, your customers, and reward them. Treat them like human beings. Treat them the way that you want to be treated, and you will be very successful. Curate great content, have user-generated content. Get yourself a camera, use your iPhone if you've got it. Put that camera on, get a mic, figure out iMovie or another editing piece of software and make it happen. You can do it. You absolutely can do it. And guess what? It's not expensive. Anybody can do this, whether you're a large business or you're a one-man army. You can make this happen. Great content will definitely set your business up for success. And you can put it on YouTube. You can create value-added information on iTunes, through podcasts, to get that platform. You can create ebooks that help highlight the information you want to provide your consumers. Use it for lead generation. Use Amazon Kindle publishing network (it's remarkably easy to use) and drive traffic there – become a #1 bestseller overnight. There's so much you can do to provide great content, a great experience for your customer, to build yourself as an authoritative figure in the industry. Own the industry, and profit.

> *"Get yourself a camera, use your iPhone if you've got it. Put that camera on, get a mic, figure out iMovie or another editing piece of software and make it happen. You can do it!"*

And guess what? This model, you can duplicate it. You can duplicate it for any business. Okay, well as always, I'll put some resources up on themarketerscommute.com/resources page. I will have links out to curation software that you can use, examples of the 10x10x4 strategy, as well as links on how to develop your Kindle book, on how to develop a good content strategy. Find the niche, go after it, build great content, treat your customers and fans like a million bucks with a great experience and you'll be laughing. That's how easy it is.

Chapter 17

Affiliate Marketing

Affiliate marketing is known as a dirty word among some marketing professionals. Less so with up-and-coming entrepreneurs and marketers, but people in the industry – as a professional marketer, getting paid as a marketer – they really look down on affiliate marketing. And I'm going to tell you something – don't be a naysayer! It's great. Don't look down at it. It works. And a lot of people make a lot of money – millions of dollars in fact – doing affiliate marketing. Some people just don't do anything else but affiliate marketing and have a brilliant lifestyle, a lifestyle that most people would envy, where they can just walk to their pool as their commute, you know what I mean? It's really something special that you could have too if you pursued it.

> *"A lot of people make a lot of money – millions of dollars in fact – doing affiliate marketing."*

Affiliate marketing, what is it? It's all about relationships at the end of day. It's about giving to get. You're leveraging a network of publishers who have either email lists, great websites with a lot of traffic, whatever it is, and they promote your offer. They promote your product or service and for that, when you sell something as a result of that referred traffic to your site and after a successful conversion, they get a percentage of the sale. You give them 10%, 20%, 50%, 75%, whatever it is that makes sense for your business.

> *"Affiliates… they promote your product or service and for that, when you sell something as a result of the referred traffic to your site and after a successful conversion, they get a percentage of the sale."*

There is a more traditional approach to affiliate marketing, and then there's more of a secret affiliate marketing tactic, like the underworld of affiliate marketing that's really, really profitable. Affiliate marketing works really well, and it did for one brand that we probably all know, which is Amazon.com. So Amazon built their business really through the Amazon Associates program, which is affiliate marketing. Somebody would basically sign up to be an Amazon Associate, find whatever products they want to put on their website, or books they want to promote, whatever it might be. And then they would put it on their site, or put it in an email, and then if anybody clicked on it and bought it, they would get a commission. They would get on average about 10%. That's how Amazon drove a lot of traffic to their site; the associate program. So they really brought affiliate marketing to the mainstream. Some people make a good living doing it now. It's very competitive, but still a lot of people are successful at the Amazon Associates program.

Now on the product side, there is Commission Junction, Link Share, there used to be Google Affiliates that's no longer in existence, and there's some other ones as well. And they're more expensive so if you're an established brand, maybe a mid-sized company and you have a product, I would recommend that you look at those guys. They're best of breed, there's a lot of service fees, but they have huge publisher networks – I mean big brands work with them. You'll be very happy. If you can afford them, they'll do great work for you. Commissions typically are a bit lower for the publishers – it's 15% or so, really it's up to you as the brand owner. I highly recommend using them. You only pay for conversion, and of course there's service fees to the networks. Basically what they do is… they are like a broker. They have a relationship with all the vendors – you're a vendor – and then they say, "Okay we have a relationship with all these publishers, all these websites. Here's who we recommend fits for your brand. You can choose whomever you want. Just publish your offer. It's good. And then put the tracking code on the site. Go!" And then you pay your percentage as you convert a sale.

"Amazon built their business really through the Amazon Associates program, which is affiliate marketing."

I don't want to talk too much about that because, frankly, that's out of reach for most people. Unless, like I said, you're a marketer or an owner of a medium-sized to a larger organization, and you can afford to pay thousands of dollars in service fees, that's for you. But if you're like most people who have a small brand, or a digital product, maybe it's your first product you've made and you're really wondering how do you get money, how do you drive sales for this thing without breaking the bank on advertising? Well, the answer is affiliate marketing.

"If you're like most people who have a small brand, or a digital product, maybe it's your first product you've made and you're really wondering how do you get money, how do you drive sales for this thing without breaking the bank on advertising? Well, the answer is affiliate marketing."

With affiliate marketing you got to give to get. Now the key with this is you need to know how much you can afford to pay. So there's a calculation called cost per acquisition, and you can get to that number multiple different ways: What's the cost per visitor to your website? How many impressions is it? What's your conversion rate? All those things... How much have you spent? To get your cost per acquisition.

> *"You need to know how much you can afford to pay. So there's a calculation called cost per acquisition."*

Now, I actually have a calculator, a spreadsheet I built, that you can get from my website at http://themarketerscommute.com/resources. I did it for Google AdWord buying, but it's got a CPA calculation on there. And you'll be able to figure out what it is. So basically, this is all a cost per acquisition is: how much are you willing to pay to acquire a customer? So if my product is $100. Let's just say it's a digital good – I'm selling a How To Start A Business ebook course. Maybe it's five ebooks, step-by-step that guides you through it at $100. Well my cost of goods sold is $0. It doesn't cost me anything to transmit the documents electronically. I might have a processing fee, let's just say a couple percent. So if you do that, maybe have a $2 cost of goods. So what am I willing to pay somebody to promote my brand and have that customer convert? I might be willing to pay $70. I might pay somebody $70 to promote my brand, and if somebody converts, I'll give them $70. Why? Well, it's $30 for me, it's $28 I never had and I'm likely to get really high quality publishers who are really going to really work hard to try to promote that offer.

> *"I actually have a calculator, a spreadsheet I built, that you can get from my website at darrencontardo.net/resources... it's got a CPA calculation on there. And you'll be able to figure out what it is."*

Okay, well, how do you find those publishers if you're not going to use those big services like Commission Junction and Link Share? Great question. If you're a digital good, there's ClickBank. ClickBank is the #1 platform for digital good distribution and sales focusing on affiliate marketing. They even have the ClickBank Powered system, where they'll actually run your site for you, your whole sales funnel, everything, help promote your brand, all the order processing is done through ClickBank. That's great. I will tell you this though: building a site, putting an affiliate offer out there, and putting it on ClickBank is kind of like building the Field of Dreams. Just because you put a website out there, and a product, and you set up your shopping cart, and you put it on ClickBank doesn't mean it's going to sell. You have a better chance of it being a really high payout, but unless you're promoting it somehow, it's really not going to pick up. So how do you get the pickups? How do you get noticed?

"If you're a digital good, there's ClickBank. ClickBank is the #1 platform for digital good distribution and sales focusing on affiliate marketing... it doesn't mean it's going to sell... unless you're promoting it somehow."

Well, ClickBank has the marketplace you can advertise in. It's a few hundred bucks, depending what you're willing to spend. It's kind of like a CPM model. The way to go about this is to go after joint venture brokers: JV brokers is what they are typically called. And you can actually set up these contracts through ClickBank as they offer that service. And a joint venture broker is your conduit to all the publishers. They have the list of all the publishers and basically you go to them and say, "Okay JV broker, I'm going to give you 5% of sales, 10% of sales through your network for up to a year, and I'm going to give your publishers whatever it is... maybe it's $60 at this point, or $63 depending on the math. I'm still working at a $70 mark. So your total payout might be $70, 10% of that will go to the JV broker. Now you're willing to give those publishers $63. They'll say, "Okay Darren, that works." And he goes out and promotes your brand, your product offering to his network. Because now say you have a one-to-many, he is the broker, he owns it, he might say, "Okay Darren, let's put together a presentation, we'll do a webinar, we'll get everybody excited about it, and then we'll roll the sucker out." Then you go put up your landing page, you put up your site, you go through the JV broker, you do the launch emails, you provide him with the creative, the banner ads, the email copy, everything they need to be successful. And then you sit back, you launch it, and you wait for those orders to come in.

> *"ClickBank has the marketplace you can advertise in... The way to go about this is to go after joint venture brokers. And you can actually set up these contracts through ClickBank as they offer that service."*

Now if you really want to make money, if you're really serious about this, what you need to do is you need to set up your sales funnel appropriately. So I talked about this $100 offer, right? That's fine, you'll definitely get people going on that, but what I'd recommend you do in order to really be successful here is look at your sales funnel. Your sales funnel should be a 3-, even sometimes a 4-step process. And typically if you want the best conversion rate, uptick on your initial offer, I'd recommend a free offer. Sounds scary to most people. Or maybe even a really low, low-cost offer, like $10, $20, maybe even $50. This gets people in the top of your sales funnel. Most people will go after this and you got to make sure the payout is high.

> *"Now if you really want to make money, you need to set up your sales funnel appropriately. Your sales funnel should be a 3-, even sometimes a 4-step process. I'd recommend a free offer."*

Let's use the free offer as an example (this works for physical goods as well). You offer the product for free and after somebody converts, you have an email follow-up system that's maybe 3, 4, emails sent out on a daily, maybe every 2 day basis, that really talk about the value added service that you provide, value added to whatever your initial free offering was. And then you start talking about your next product that they should buy. You just kind of put it in there a little bit. And that would be your… maybe membership site. Your membership site might be maybe $20 a month.

Now, why would you want to do that? Well, you already paid for the lead through this free offering. You are willing to give a cost per acquisition for that free lead. And then you want to convert them on your membership, and your membership is a recurring fee, so that is monthly. So now you're starting to get into profitability.

> *"You already paid for the lead through this free offering… then you want to convert them on your membership, and your membership is a recurring fee, so that is monthly. So now you're starting to get into profitability."*

Then after people subscribe to your membership… now less people will…. like let's just say 100% of people are on your free offer, you might have only 50% or less that take your membership, but you're going to get money every month. Now you're starting to build a pipeline of cash, now you're building a system here. Those people you want to have email follow-ups with and then start eventually promoting your bigger offer. It might be a mastermind group, where you get on a call with people or they get select access to you for your system. In this case, I'll be talking about a business development system. Then you could do a call for 30 minutes once a week – insider information nobody else has access to, elite level training, sharing stories and tactics and strategies amongst the group as a mastermind. And people love this because it really holds them accountable, they meet new people and they grow. That price point might be $500, it might be $1000. And yes, you'll have less people take you up on this, but think about it. Now all of a sudden, you got everybody in on your free offer. You got maybe half of those people on a membership with recurring monthly income coming in, and then a percentage of those – maybe it's 5% – who take your $1000 mastermind program. That's pretty good.

"Ladder up your customer in your sales funnel to maximize profit in the long-run with great cashflow."

Now you're getting the money. So you might figure out, "Okay, I'm willing to pay that $70 for initial customer acquisition because I know I'm going to be profitable through the customer lifetime value of that individual. If your average customer lifetime value ends up being something like $500, on average, then absolutely you're going to pay $70 up front.

That's how this system works. Beachbody does this – you know, P90X. Everybody's heard of P90X. That's their model. They basically will take a loss initially with their DVD workout program and then they'll up sell you on bigger ticket items. They will try to get you on a monthly continuity program, like a membership, and then they'll try to sell you other things on the back end, some big ticket items. Even things like getting certified at P90X, for example. There are different things like that to continue to increase their customer lifetime value. They're very intelligent in how they do it. They're a billion dollar company. It's quite phenomenal.

"Pay that $70 for initial customer acquisition. If your average customer lifetime value ends up being something like

$500, on average, then absolutely you're going to pay $70 up front."

You too can use the same system to a lesser scale with your digital products. You can use this for physical products. Now, you can't use ClickBank for physical products, but there are programs out there, there are affiliate marketing brokers that will do physical products. W4 is a great one. W4.com is a great boutique service that will only charge you a CPA fee; they will not charge you a monthly fee. So if you say okay, say you're selling diet pills, and those diet pills… you're willing to pay a $50 cost per acquisition. You're giving away a free trial, but at the end of that free trial, if somebody doesn't return that product, you bill them, and then they have to get them on that continuity program. You know, you ship product every month. And all of a sudden, that's kind of like your membership fee. See the similarities? Say you're charging $50, $80 a month on recurring revenue until they cancel. Then what you want to do, just like our digital good model is when you're communicating with them and sending them follow-up emails, you know, up sell them to something bigger. Maybe you have a cleanse product, maybe you have a whole nutrition program that you can sell them as well. All these things to make that basket bigger, thus increasing your LTV. That's what you always want to think about. I get them in with a great, sweet offer. I grow them. I keep them and I grow them and then it's all about the life-time value. So with those calculations, you'll figure out what your cost per acquisition is, what you're willing to pay for. And as long as your CPA is less than your lifetime value and you have profit left in, you can do that all day long.

"I get them in with a great, sweet offer. I grow them. I keep them and then it's all about the lifetime value… And as long

your CPA is less than your lifetime value and you have profit left in, you can do that all day long."

Here is something you need to do first. You need to figure out what you're willing to pay before you get into a JV broker situation. Basically, you got to go in and build up your sales funnel, your offer, your main offer. In this case, it could be that freebie we're talking about. And you need to do some paid advertising. I know – we talked about affiliate marketing is a great way not to have to pay unless you sell something, which is pay for performance, which I'm a huge fan of, which is what I'm talking about here. But you have to prove that your product will sell – or service – that it will sell. And the way to do that is you got to buy some Google AdWords, or you do Facebook ads or Twitter ads, some direct response type traffic to your landing page with that offer and measure your conversion rate.

If your conversion rate is below 1%, you're going to have a hard time attracting a joint venture broker. They're going to say… first thing they ask you when you approach them is they say "Okay, what's your conversion rate?" If you don't know, they won't take you. If it's below 1%, it's going to be a tough sell. Because the next question is going to be "What's your average order amount?" If you don't know, you're screwed. If you know, and it's high, then that's great. If it's a free offer, you can say, "Well, my conversion rate is whatever it is… 2%, 3%. It's a free offer, but my back-end sales are $100. I'm willing to pay you $70."

"If your conversion rate is below 1%, you're going to have a hard time attracting a joint venture broker."

For your test, you need to figure this out. So you build that landing page with that offer, you drive your paid traffic to it, whether it's Facebook dark posts, Twitter direct response ads, with website cards, or Google

AdWords. You point those people to your offer, and then you look at the traffic you got, and how many people converted, and that's your conversion rate. Then you look at how many people took your second offer. How to do that is you have to set up an email auto-responder through Aweber, or MailChimp, or Get Response, or Exact Target, or whatever email system you're using. That's the best way to do it. You get them, say, "Thank you for your email. Here's your order. Thank you for your order." And then you send the series of emails. And eventually you send out the follow-up offer… which is boom, going for the second membership offer, whatever that might be.

> *"For your test, you need to figure this out. So you build that landing page with that offer, you drive your paid traffic to it, whether it's Facebook dark posts, Twitter direct response ads, with website cards, or Google AdWords."*

If you know that, and how long they stay in the membership – and you might want to test this out for a few months – you'll be able to know. And you'll say, "Well JV broker, my conversion rate is 2%, my average order amount is x dollars, my retention rate is x dollars. I'm willing to give you $50, $60, $70 on a cost per acquisition." He'll say, "Great, let's get this thing moving." And you're off to the races. If you don't have those pieces of information already identified, unless you're a great speaker and can convince these people to take action with you – you're going to be SOL.

That's what you really need to do to really lure in and attract a JV broker. You just don't want to waste their time. If you were them, you wouldn't want to waste your time with a dog of an offer. You want to know the product or service sells and that you can make money at it, and that the publishers will make money at it. These are busy people who are very successful. They are very efficient with their time. But they can make a huge, huge business for you. I've met a couple JV brokers that can just kill it. They have literally added millions of dollars to some brands.

Where do you find these people? You can find them on JV Zoo. JV Zoo is also an alternative to ClickBank. There's a couple on there… JV Zoo is more for like digital goods that are more business oriented, you know like SEO firmware, WordPress themes, those kinds of things. WarriorForum.com is an ideal place to find joint venture brokers. There's a lot of Facebook groups out there too for JV brokers, and ad network shares and stuff like that. Look at Facebook groups, you can definitely find them on there. Obviously, you can just go to Google and find them. There's a few that are really good and there's a lot that are decent. So you have to do your homework on it. They really make a huge difference. Just remember you have to test. You have to find out what your conversion rate is. You have to experiment with your offer, your creative, your landing page, and your bid. You have to experiment with your up sells. Are you doing the membership or just the larger second-tier offering? Do you have no idea what to do if you don't? If you have a digital good, consider the ClickBank Powered store to really set things up automatically, make it easier on yourself.

> *"Where do you find these people? JV Zoo. JV Zoo is more for like digital goods that are more business oriented, you know like SEO firmware, WordPress themes, those kinds of things. WarriorForum.com is an ideal place to find joint venture brokers. There's a lot of Facebook groups out there too."*

And also remember too that affiliate networks and affiliate marketing is so successful and drives so much traffic, that your merchant provider is going to wonder what's going on. And they'll probably shut you down if you don't let them know what's happening. Even PayPal has done that to people. So be aware of that. You want to protect yourself because the worst thing is you might have an offer going on and all of a sudden your merchant account gets shut down and you can't process orders, and affiliates aren't getting paid, and your JV broker's not getting paid. Man, that's going to be a really bad situation – you definitely want to avoid that.

I've covered pretty much everything so far in affiliate marketing. I really recommend you go after this as your first channel if you're just starting out. Like I said, do your tests first and then go after the affiliate space. You'll be so thankful that you did. You can really change your life. And you don't have to pay unless it's performing. So it's really a great opportunity for you to really grow your business, have fun, and prosper.

Chapter 18

Email Marketing & List Building

We've touched on this a little bit in other chapters but email marketing and list building deserves more attention. Email marketing is truly one of the most effective ways to build a business. It allows you to connect with your customers and have a conversation with them. Everyone talks about social and how crucial it is and yes I agree, absolutely, but you have to ask yourself the question, *What are you trying to achieve?* With Facebook for example, 1-2% of the posts you put out there get seen by your audience. You have to boost posts; it costs money. You can do unpublished posts (dark posts) to do some A/B testing but that's not the purpose of this chapter. This chapter is about what IS going to get seen. What IS being delivered to their inbox. What IS going to build authority, a relationship, and loyalty. That's email marketing.

Email is still the #1 killer app. It's extremely powerful and very inexpensive; you can't go wrong with it. There are a lot of email service providers out there. I've used Aweber which is fantastic for small or medium sized businesses, primarily focused on small business or info-entrepreneur. I currently use it and you can do a lot with it. You can develop web forms with just the click of a button; you don't need any design experience to import images and make it look great.

"Email is still the #1 killer app. It's extremely powerful and very inexpensive; you can't go wrong with it."

Then there are tools like MailChimp, which is also used for various sized businesses. You can set up three emails for lists up to 500 so if you're just starting out, and you don't want to pay for it I'd highly recommend MailChimp just so you can get out there and get some experience with email marketing. You're not going to get the full host of features with the autoresponder but it's still very effective. There are other tools out there like Vertical Response, Drip, Email Direct (which is good for the advanced marketer). In this chapter I want to talk about the tools available to you, the creative within the email itself – the copywriting and strategies for the best response rate – and list building, which is so powerful. The businesses that have the biggest list, win. The bigger the list, the bigger the business. I've seen it happen many times in my career. I've built a list from nothing to almost 250k in six months using good, solid, tactical maneuvers.

"The bigger the list, the bigger the business. I've seen it happen many times in my career. I've built a list from nothing to almost 250k in six months using good, solid, tactical maneuvers."

Before we get into that let's talk about the tools. I've mentioned Aweber, MailChimp, and others. Your goal here is to develop a lead, so you might have a free ebook or other lead magnet. Imagine this: if you go for the sale right away. Let's say you've done a Facebook direct ad urging someone to buy now for an info product or you have a service and you want them to buy right away. Stop wasting your money; it's difficult. Instead invest in building a relationship and create a free lead product value exchange. Give that prospect something of value for their email address. A report, a free white paper, a free ebook or some kind of teaser. Give them a lead product to get them in the door; something someone will subscribe to to receive. Always think about what you can do to help them on their journey. In that collateral you want to position yourself as an authority. Then when you get their email address you want to have an autoresponder. Set that up in Aweber or MailChimp.

> *"Stop wasting your money… Invest in building a relationship and create a free lead product value exchange. Give that prospect something of value for their email address. A report, a free white paper, a free ebook or some kind of teaser."*

Once that prospect enters their email for that freebie they'll get an automatic double opt in. This is important because it's all about return on investment; you don't want bots just filling in the forms. You'll have a higher conversion rate if you cross your t's and dot your i's right now. Your ego may take a beating because some may not take the double opt in but when they do you know they're committed. Then they'll get the follow up email with the PDF. If you're delivering a white paper PDF and you're concerned about the server load, you can host it on Amazon S3 network for free up to a certain point. I've done that myself and it's efficient. You can put security measures on so it can't be passed around.

> *"Once that prospect enters their email for that freebie they'll get an automatic double opt in. This is important because it's all about return on investment; you don't want bots just filling in the forms."*

So that's your lead generation. Then you want to do another value add email. You want to start that conversation using the autoresponders. So in whatever app you're using, set the rule up that the thank you email with download is sent immediately. Then two days later you're sending another value added email. "Hi Joe, to help you further choose the right _____, here are things to watch out for and be aware of." Giving them more value. NO call to action; don't ask for a thing. Then another two days later you're sending another email with more value added info. Something else to help build the relationship. Maybe add some testimonials in there too, someone who used your service and had something good to say about it. Two days after this, send another value added email. We're talking three value adds here. Things to look out for, how you can help them. Does this sound familiar? We covered some of this in the marketing automation chapter, but it's so powerful it's worth diving into again.

You've gotta give to get and you have to have the mindset of abundance and know that as much as you give, it'll come back. So that's your third value add email within the span of less than a week. Then you hit 'em up with your promo email – your offer. This where you ask for the money. You're offering your service and asking for a buy. Whatever your offer may be, you're calling to action. Don't be surprised if people don't take action. Just set another promo email up a day or two later, and this offer should be a little more aggressive. Free consultation plus a credit, for example. And a link to "buy now" etc. Your last promotional email, your third email, will be a really hard sell. Your rock bottom deal. Offer them something great, something zero risk (e.g. I only get paid "if" email).

"You've gotta give to get and you have to have the mindset of abundance and know that as much as you give, it'll come back."

This allows you to have a powerful offer that you've built a relationship for, and you can convert them. This strategy works exceptionally well.

I've used it, I'm telling you it works. Autoresponders work; you can sit down and map it out over the course of a day. You develop these emails and you can send it out over the predetermined schedule, while your prospect thinks you're sending these emails daily to them… allowing them to build a relationship with them to "warm them up" before a larger buy.

> *"Autoresponders work; you can sit down and map it out over the course of a day."*

Then there's the question of HTML vs TEXT emails. HTML looks beautiful, but it's not personal because just as when you send a friend an email you write it in plain text, your email marketing should be the same way. Plus, it's low tech and you don't have to spend the time with designers, not the money to get a gorgeous looking email out the door. Besides, download times are longer with HTML and some email spam filters will strip your images out before they are downloaded so the email doesn't even get read. Additionally, with TEXT emails your hyperlinks stand out clearly as a call to action because of the blue color links for the text, which we are all used to seeing. I've done both types of email and I've spent more time optimizing HMTL emails and the results between the two types are more favorable to TEXT anyway.

> *"I've spent more time optimizing HMTL emails and the results between the two types are more favorable to TEXT anyway."*

Now the most important thing in your email is your copywriting (we're writing text right)? And, as you can imagine the absolute #1 thing to focus on is your subject line. After all, if your prospect doesn't open your email then your offer won't be purchased. Great strategies to use in your email subject should help spark curiosity to solve a problem for them, such as asking questions like "How to win your court case", or "Discover that one secret to increasing your case file success rate". Another great tactic is to use number in your subject line, just like you see on magazine covers… "21 ways to win cases fast, revealed". My experience is those types of subject lines get multiples in open rates above standard emails. You can A/B split test your subject lines to see for yourself within your email provider.

> *"Now the most important thing in your email is your copywriting… the absolute #1 thing to focus on is your subject line."*

The next thing to focus on is the "From:" in your email. I highly recommend using your name or at least someone's name instead of "ABC corp" because it creates the personal touch while building a relationship. Make it transparent and authentic to help satisfy your prospect's desire for human interaction. That's where the dopamine rush comes in; getting an email from a friend. After all, every business is people to people, not business to people. In fact, I've done this before myself many times even with big brands. I put an athletes name in the FROM and emailed my list of 250,000 subscribers for them to attend a tradeshow and to get an autograph and/or a picture. The results were phenomenal, I received more than double the open rate while having a successful tradeshow. Imagine for example if you received an email from Michael Jordan to come out to a Bull's game back when he was playing vs from The Chicago Bulls. I'm sure you would open it, take a look, probably even print it and frame it up on your wall! That's the power of personalization.

> *"Imagine for example if you received an email from Michael Jordan to come out to a Bull's game back when he was playing vs from The Chicago Bulls. I'm sure you would open it, take a look, probably even print it and frame it up on your wall!"*

As I mentioned earlier, if you're not sure what email subject line to go with you can turn to A/B split testing. A/B split testing allows you to create two variables in your email marketing to try to maximize your open rate and your click through rate. All you do is set up the same email twice, change the subject line and direct a decent sample size (about 300) of your list to each email with the use of your hyperlinks. The best performer now becomes your main email to send to your entire list. Now, you can even go a step further and A/B the content inside your email after your subject line is chosen. Here repeat the process again, watch for the best CTR, then make that email your master email you send to the rest of your list. This process mitigates the risk and maximizes the reward… it will make you more money, guaranteed!

> *"If you're not sure what email subject line to go with you can turn to A/B split testing. A/B split testing allows you to create two variables in your email marketing to try to maximize your open rate and your click through rate."*

Remember to make your creative work hard, use guarantees, scarcity, testimonials, and a strong call to action. Using these tactics in a logical order will get you results, just like it has for me. Think of these pieces as a puzzle, they all fit together, so spend the time to make it work – it will be worth it.

Now onto list building, the critical component to breaking free as an entrepreneur and elevating your game as a marketer. List building will require you to get a good landing page that has a webform on it where you can link into to your email marketing software. I recommend tools like Leadpages.net, Unbounce, Clickfunnels, and OptimizePress (wordpress theme) for your landing page. For email marketing tools I recommend Drip (works natively with Leadpages), Aweber, Mailchimp, and Clickfunnels. Landing pages by nature don't have global navigation at the top of the page because the primary goal is for you to convert your prospect from your traffic source to your list. All the landing page template software listed above will give you the best landing pages for the type of goal you have, so in some cases video will work better or a long page with scrolling that tells the Star, Story, and Solution narrative (that's where you have a main character who had an epiphany, overcame something, arrived at the solution and now makes it available to the audience).

> *"List building will require you to get a good landing page that has a webform on it where you can link into to your email marketing software."*

In order for your landing page to really convert, you have to consider the right audience and make the content as contextual as possible. The best way to do this is to ensure some of the copy points in the ad are on the headline and copy points of the landing page. Additionally, if you targeted your audience on Facebook you need to realize that those prospects are cold and top of funnel so you're going to need several contact points before they're ready to buy, after all their mindset on Facebook is leisure and social. The opposite is true for search; that audience is actively looking to solve a problem and if your widget can help they are more likely to convert and require less touch points. This is an important distinction when considering your landing page and email integration. With your search campaign and your Facebook ads insert a tracking pixel on the landing page and your thank you page so you can measure your conversions, insert those pages into your GOAL sequence on Google Analytics as well to close the loop. Now you can measure your success and optimize your ROI (incremental sales – incremental costs/incremental costs).

"If you targeted your audience on Facebook you need to realize that those prospects are cold and top of funnel so you're going to need several contact points before they're ready to buy, after all their mindset on Facebook is leisure and social."

You may not know this, but there are FREE list building strategies that work as well, and you should be using them immediately. The most effective way to build your list is to find complementary services/companies that could benefit from a relationship with you. For example, using our lawyer example you would connect with a real estate agent and mail each other's list offering your services or have them email their list with a referral to you, which is even better. It's best to sweeten the pot with an offer exclusive to their list such as a free consultation in this example. Another great example would be partner with a moving company or really any other company that is complementary to your service. This is actually how affiliates build their list, the difference is they take a cut of your sales. Just remember, it's best to have a customized landing page with your offer and a subsequent email campaign that closes the loop on the sale for you, allowing you to see your conversation rates. Then once you close the sale ask for your list to refer you to new customers and repeat the process again. You can see how powerful this strategy is and just how low cost it is.

"There are FREE list building strategies that work... The most effective way to build your list is to find complementary services/companies that could benefit from a relationship with you."

I actually did a campaign with MapMyRide a few years ago when they were promoting The Tour de France and I simply called them up, said I wanted to email their list an offer and vice versa. They agreed and it cost me a few hundred bucks to get the landing page up, the emails set up, and the cost of my product… I got tens of thousands of subscribers from that campaign and it was dirt cheap. This shows you how you can easily do it yourself with a tremendously low cost per acquisition.

What about taking this another step further? You can offer a FREE report (using our lawyer example again) called "21 Steps to Have a Low Cost Divorce" that is posted on your business card, your signature on your email, your stationary, your social feeds, or anything else for that matter in a form of a landing page. The page could be "lowcostdivorce.com/freereport" or whatever you deem necessary. Now you have all your existing pieces of collateral working hard for you at building your email list as "bait" to get new prospects into your sales funnel. Even if you did just one thing it would be to stop directing folks to your home page on your website. It's a waste of time unless you have an offer right there to get them into your sales funnel. Furthermore, once someone becomes a customer through your sales funnel, move them to a new email customer list. This list can be emailed to grow your existing customer revenue with new offers just like a bank does (credit card >> checking account >> car loan >> mortgage >> 401k >> etc). You can do this automatically as a rule through Aweber and other email list management tools.

> *"Even if you did just one thing it would be to stop directing folks to your home page on your website. It's a waste of time unless you have an offer right there to get them into your sales funnel."*

To demonstrate the power of email, I created an offer to my existing list and offered them free shipping on any order of $50 or more, emailed 130,000 people and generated an incremental $5000 of sales in one day. The email cost was $700, so the return on ad spend was 3.5… I know that as long as I can get a 3:1 return then the profit line is in good shape. Depending on your cost structure it may be more or less, but you see how quickly you can generate incremental sales with your list. It is without a doubt the MOST IMPORTANT THING TO YOUR BUSINESS TO SUCCEED.

> *"I created an offer to my existing list and offered them free shipping on any order of $50 or more, emailed 130,000 people and generated an incremental $5,000 of sales in one day. The email cost was $700, so the return on ad spend was 3.5."*

Back in the early 2000's I was leading the digital marketing team for a leading MuscleTech. We didn't have an email list or even an email marketing solution, so we chose Vertical ResponseÒ. They are a great system that even links up post cards for an email to direct mail program that has solid conversion rates. So at that time we didn't have our list, got set up with them and opted to start building our list using a single opt-in strategy. This won't work today, but back then CAN-SPAM didn't exist so it was compliant. When we launched we put the opt in form on our webpage, offered free reports on how to add an inch to your arms in 24 hours, build a better body, eat right for gains, etc. The result was we built our list from zero to 250,000 people in 6 months. The other strategy I used to build the list was to always ask my list to forward their email on to their friends so they could get the free report too. Basically, I turned my list into my marketing team and it worked. I would average about 5% list growth every email send from this referral program. It's a great tactic to use on your email that I suggest you use too. However, the BIGGEST SECRET to success that I used to grow the list was to have one field for prospects to enter their email address on the homepage, so it seemed like a simple task for them, then once they hit submit, they would go to another page where their email address was prepopulated and other fields were there to finish the subscribe process (I had about 7 fields).

> *"The BIGGEST SECRET to success that I used to grow the list was to have one field for prospects to enter their email address on the homepage, so it seemed like a simple task for them."*

The psychology behind this is incredibly powerful; people already feel committed to the process of subscribing and are far more likely to finish the process than they would be if faced with the 7 fields on the form right at sign up in the first place. This tactic gave me double digit subscribe conversion rates and I highly recommend you use it on your site to grow your list fast. So where do you put the form? I put it above the fold on the site, as the main call to action below the slider, and again later on each page on the side navigation, and at the bottom of each blog post. By doing all of the above we drove zero in sales to over $1,000,000 in about three years, again this was in early 2000 before people bought online every day.

> *"We drove zero in sales to over $1,000,000 in about three years, again this was in early 2000 before people bought online every day."*

I don't care if you're a one-man army or a big business, email list building is by far the most effective thing you can do to build your business. Far more important than building a Facebook fan page with a bunch of followers who don't convert. Spend your time on profit producing email marketing and list building. Done properly email can provide a 47:1 ROI. It's the way of the past, the present, and the way of the future. Get on it fast and build your business or continue to struggle.

Chapter 19

Direct Response Facebook & Twitter Ads That Work

My belief in marketing is that there are levels of expertise in marketing; generalists like brand marketers create or evoke emotional responses to their brand that is extremely visual, repetitive, and it's very creative. However, it's very difficult to measure it an a very fragmented world. Especially hard to measure in the digital ecosystem. The other side to that, where I think the experts live, is in direct response marketing. Now depending on who you talk to you that opinion will be shared and will be polarized to the extreme and adamantly opposed. At the end of the day you have to ask yourself an important question: Do I want to sell stuff and make my money work hard or do I want to feed my ego, potentially win awards, and have the money to fund it.

Don't get me wrong, great creative based off of valuable insight is the secret ingredient to making either method work and without it, no matter what you choose, you'll miss the mark and the sales just won't be there. The right insight with the right target audience, with the right message, and the right time is the key. At least with direct response you can see if your audience actually opens up their wallet to purchase.

If you want to test a concept or idea with traditional brand advertising, you'll have to first do a qualitative study to get the insight, then follow up with quantitative studies to ensure enough of the population in your sample size believes it appeals to them. At the end of the day do you want to move the needle and sell products fast? If so go with at least a direct response test because even with all the testing, consumers often tell you one thing and do another. So much so, that in my career I've spent hundreds of thousands on market research to see if a product would resonate and sell to the target audience, did a whole rollout at retail, spent an additional hundreds of thousands of dollars a week during the launch phase and it fell totally flat. I had a celebrity selling the product on package, in TV, on print, and all tests said it was a home run. Yet the sales were the worst I've ever seen.

So what did I do? I funded a DR test; one with my celebrity and one without. The offer was the same, the message was the same, but the only difference is one had a celebrity and one didn't. The creative without the celebrity performed better, so immediately the campaign and product was cancelled. All money was reallocated to different brands, the celebrity had his contract closed out early, and the brand was marked down at retail. What's the lesson? Test in DR before betting the farm on old-school testing.

> *"At the end of the day do you want to move the needle and sell products fast? If so go with at least a direct response test because, even with all the testing, consumers often tell you one thing and do another!"*

So how much should you spend to launch a product? I suggest somewhere between 20-30% of sales to rapidly launch the brand or product/service. Where you spend this can change of course, but if you want to get traction either via pure play DR or at retail you'll need to be in that ball park. Over time you can decrease your percentage and increase your profit margin. I do recommend DR though because even though the heyday in DR was in the 90's with TV where guys selling the knives that cut through cans (who were selling over 50,000 units a week), or the Chia PetÒ, the new frontier is upon us with Facebook, Twitter, and of course Google.

Before we get into detail on the direct response aspects of the digital world I want to go through more of the economics of marketing. The Media Efficiency Ratio or MER is a metric to measure return on ad spend, so for every dollar spend in advertising what you make in sales, some refer to this a ROAS or Return On Ad Spend. Where this gets exciting is if you have a retail presence. It could be national, regional, or even local for that matter.

Imagine you do an ad with an offer online that directs to your on-line store and you target your audience, they buy online, but yet they also buy offline at retail. Even though you didn't have a call to action to buy at retail. So typically a profitable MER in direct response is 3.5 or more. If you have retail sales that only increases your ratio and of course your profit. Now you may be thinking that retailers would be upset if you sold your item direct and didn't tag them or tell the consumer to buy with them. Wrong! Retailers understand that advertising still drives traffic to retail and that a smart direct response marketer will end up spending more in the long term because they can – their model allows for it! Even more powerful is that typically for every unit purchased direct, there are 10 purchased at retail. Now this is a national average with national distribution, but the relationship should still hold within a local market. So in essence what you're doing here is "cheating the system" and getting the upper hand on regular brand marketers. Now you can build your brand and make money the whole time. However, that model isn't for everyone if you don't have funds for TV or a retail presence, but don't get discouraged! You can get into the game by using internet marketing and the Facebook, Twitter, and Google ads I mentioned earlier.

"Retailers understand that advertising still drives traffic to retail and that a smart direct response marketer will end up spending more in the long term because they can – their model allows for it! Even more powerful is that typically for every unit purchased direct, there are 10 purchased at retail."

With internet-based direct response ads you can eliminate your risk, test and optimize ads at low costs, get a merchant account easily, and choose from many different payment solutions based on your needs. You can even use pay-for-performance marketing via affiliate marketing to drive your business growth, which is a form of direct response ads. Plus you can get up and running in days with all of this.

"With internet-based direct response ads you can eliminate your risk, test and optimize ads at low costs."

In particular, Facebook and Twitter have come on strong as of late to focus their ad network on direct response ad tools to increase their ad revenue potential. This is great news for you! They have fundamentally changed the landscape with direct response marketing by unleashing hyper-targeted tools where you can target your audience down to the most psychographic level to help yield a higher MER. Fortunately for you most marketers still struggle with these platforms and make many mistakes when doing the ads and the sales funnel associated. Even better, many marketers still chase Facebook likes and post organically without boosting or using dark posts, so you can outsmart them fast. Now getting likes previously may have worked and did for me years ago before Facebook changed the algorithm and now only deliver 1-2% of the organic posts to their audience, well to your audience you paid to acquire – it really is rented land. And as with any lease they increase the price all the time. Just several years ago I got over 100,000 followers in a few weeks to launch a brand using great content and cheap follower acquisition strategies. Now those tactics don't really return.

"Most marketers still struggle with these platforms and make many mistakes when doing the ads and the sales funnel associated. Even better, many marketers still chase Facebook likes and post organically without boosting or using dark posts, so you can outsmart them fast."

What you can do today is use Facebook Dark post and boosted posts. Just like Google Adwords, there you buy based on a cost per lick or CPM, you can buy on Facebook and Twitter the same way. Truth be told I usually go to Google first to get the lower in the funnel keywords that relate to my product or service for quick wins because those consumers raised their hand and are actively looking for a product or service like yours. You can use Google Shopping as well if you have an online store for a better conversion. Take the example of dog food; if you're searching for dog food and get served up an ad for dog food then you're likely to look at it and even consider purchasing it if the price and features are right for you. That's the sweet spot for Google and nobody can touch them there, but it's limited by the demand of the brand keyword, category keyword or even competitors. Unlike Google, Twitter and Facebook have a consumer that is passively looking at their feed for entertainment, zombie-like addiction, or just to creep on their friends. So why even use social ads? Well they are great for reaching your potential consumer at the top of the funnel, where there are more of them and with great targeting you can reach the right one. The trick here is that you need the right offer for these cold contacts to convert. Not only do you need the right offer, you need the right offer sequence because these folks rarely convert on a straight ad to sale page.

"Facebook ads… you need the right offer for these cold contacts to convert. Not only do you need the right offer, you need the right offer sequence because these folks rarely convert on a straight ad to sale page."

To create Facebook ads properly you'll need to download the Power Editor from Facebook in their ads section and that can only be used in Google Chrome. Why you want to do this is you'll want to use Facebook Dark posts also known as unpublished posts to reach your core audience and the difference between those ads and others you can do within Facebook is that dark posts don't show up on your feed. You'll also need a brand page for your business to do this. Dark posts have changed the game for DR because you can target people who don't like your page, like your competitors page, who are interested in your product category, that live within your distribution region, and have a propensity to buy online (so you can ensure your online sales will be there too). The magic with Facebook though is look-a-like audience – if you're not using them, you're missing out!

Anybody that comes to your website, you can cookie them and serve up ads to them on Facebook with re-targeting, and you can upload your email list to Facebook and then Facebook will match the list to the users they have on Facebook. Then you can tell Facebook to target an audience that looks like your email list on the Facebook platform with your ads. So basically, you can build a look-a-like list with folks coming to your site, your email list, and target people that have the same behaviors, demographics, and psychographics as them. What does that mean? That means you've just increased the reach of your ideal customer!!! Facebook will tell you how big that audience is, which you can use to determine your market size and potential. Now hit them up with ads, drive them to a landing page, get a good offer going, and use a stellar email follow up sequence to convert the cold, but valuable prospect.

"You can build a look-a-like list with folks coming to your site, your email list, and target people that have the same behaviors, demographics, and psychographics as them."

Just from what I mapped out here you can set 4 different Facebook ad sequences at the same time:

1) Boost your post to existing Facebook members and folks like them on Facebook (shows up in your feed)
2) Create a re-targeting Facebook ad to folks who came to your site and didn't convert with an offer
3) Create a Facebook dark post ad to those on your look-a-like audience you uploaded from your email list and web beacon
4) Create a Facebook dark post ad to those who buy your competitors
5) Bonus Advanced Ad: Create a Facebook ad to those who purchased and haven't come back to buy with a web beacon on your thank you page (post purchase).

Here's what I did and this got me a 1000%+ ROI:

A) I went in Facebook and developed an ad for a free webinar using a custom audience (no look-a-like yet)
B) Created the dark post, and drove the ad to a landing page, that had a web form that went into my email marketing system
C) Created a series of auto responder emails tied to the promotional webinar
   1. Email 1: thanks for registering for webinar, add to your calendar
   2. Email 2: Day 2, here is the product info on what you can expect

3. Email 3: Day 3, here is more info in the webinar, can't wait to see you
4. Email 4: Day 4, reminder you're going to get great deals after the webinar
5. Email 5: Day 5, the webinar starts today at x time, don't be late space is limited
6. Email 6: Day 5, 30 min before webinar, get your seat now and come early
7. Email 7: Day 5, 5 min before webinar, starting now, you may be late, last chance
8. Email 8: Day 5, 5 min post webinar, here is your offer code for your deal and a replay of the webinar
9. Email 9: Day 5, 12 hours post webinar, you didn't buy yet here's your last chance at this deal
10. Email 10: Day 6, 24 hours post webinar, you didn't buy, so we sweetened the offer (escalated the deal with a deeper discount), but you only have 24 hours
11. Email 11: Day 7, 48 hours post webinar, Absolutely last chance with rock bottom never again offered deal, gone today

The result was outstanding and I had over 1000% ROI on the ad campaign with 11 times increase in sales!!! So what was the magic? If you haven't figured it out yet social ads only work well with a good sales funnel and you have to give to get. You have to give away great value, engage your prospect with constant contact and warm them up to the point where they will convert. More importantly you have to use direct response tactics at every point of communication to address the problem, solution, credibility, trust, social proof, scientific proof, and a strong call to action to tell them what to do in every step. You are in essence leading your prospect through a purchase funnel and they think that they are getting great value and building a relationship with you the whole time. It's a win/win! What would you do with your business if you could replicate this? What about tracking this into a LTV not just a straight ROI on the program? The results could be staggering!

"I had over 1000% ROI on the ad campaign with a 11 times increase in sales! So what was the magic? If you haven't fig-ure it out yet social ads only work well with a good sales fun-nel and you have to give to get."

If you want to drive retail or event traffic you can use Facebook ads is to use events or coupons where they can scan them on their phone in retail and geo-target them to drive sales. Then you can measure the result in nearly real time. Tough Mudder actually built their brand on Facebook and have 10,000 people going to their events at any one time, just doing this. In fact, they are the #1 obstacle brand!

Another option for direct response ads is Twitter and they have come out with a suite of tools that allow you to hyper-target your audience as well on their platform. Fortunately, most marketers don't know Twitter well, plus it's an open network that's indexed so all can see it. They now offer what they call "cards." Cards allow you to create ad units like Facebook where you can have videos and images in your ad and target by demographics, keywords, trending topics, and unlike Facebook there isn't a limit on the characters on the ads unit visual.

For example, you put the copy right on the ad, have a click on the ad, measure the conversion, and even use the email sales funnel to maxi-mize your sales. With good creative and testing you can get outstanding results. For example, I did an ad that broke Twitter's engagement rate that received a 22% engagement rate, while their engagement average was below 5%. In fact, I got a call from Twitter HQ asking me what my secret was. My response was direct response tactics mixed with value added content tied to a relevant image; I used a pro athlete on a magazine I had on contract, targeted competitors and people who liked my product, the category, or had a problem my product could solve, then did a post that explained how she used a product, drove that CTA to a blog post, where I had a call to action to buy my product. After that I started to work with Twitter to help develop and test out their new direct response ads.

> *"I did an ad that broke Twitter's engagement rate that received a 22% engagement rate, while their engagement average was below 5%. I got a call from Twitter HQ asking me what my secret was."*

You can even use Twitter to test product concepts, put vine videos into Twitter for storytelling and with a call-to-action. What these means is that you can create a concept and test with these platforms, scale once you find a winner, and grow a big business fast! No longer do big business have the upper hand; it's the smaller, nimble, and cutting-edge marketers that have the edge. *You* have the edge! The cost of entry is low, the data reliability is high and the opportunity is huge! Arriving at an opportunity where everyone is already isn't an opportunity. Arriving at an opportunity where only the few are that are doing it properly is a real opportunity. That's what you need to do… test and figure these DR platforms out. Even Walmart is asking me to help them drive traffic to their store using these tactics now, so hurry, the time is now!

Chapter 20

Sales Automation (Sales Funnels)

Have you heard of sales funnels or sales automation and aren't sure what it is? If so, then you're missing out because done properly sales automation can dramatically scale your business for growth – while you sit back and watch the cash come in. What you will need is a series of tools and software to make it happen and that's where it can get a bit tricky depending on your business needs. If you're an online entrepreneur or run an online business you can choose from Infusionsoft, Kajabi, Membergate, LeadPages, etc. What I have used is a hybrid approach using one of the most powerful marketing tools available and that's email. Yes, the not so sexy, not so hyped tool that is the first thing you check in the morning and the last thing you check at night - your moneymaker! The beauty of email is that it is personal and helps build the relationship with your prospect to the point where they're very likely to convert into a customer.

> *"Done properly sales automation can dramatically scale your business for growth – while you sit back and watch the cash come in."*

Really what sales automation or a sales funnel is is where you set up a series of communication touch points that guide the prospect through each stage of your sales steps. To do this you'll need a series of autoresponders timed over a set period to get delivered to your prospect. There is a system to use depending on what launch you're trying to do. That system contains three distinct phases; phase one is the Pre-Launch Phase, phase two is the Launch Phase, and phase three is the Post-Launch Phase.

> *"There is a system to use depending on what launch you're trying to do. That system contains three distinct phases; phase one is the Pre-Launch Phase, phase two is the Launch Phase, and phase three is the Post-Launch Phase."*

Phase 1: the Pre-Launch

In the pre-launch phase is where you can use your audience to help shape your product and make them feel like it's their own so they end up buying it and telling their friends. There are two different strategies to use within the pre-launch phase depending on if you do or don't have an existing following. If you don't have an existing following you'll have to build one, and one of the best ways is to use social media, joint venture emails, and ads. On social media one of the most effective ways is to do a Facebook Live series cloaked as a challenge where you cover your topic of your launch, so it could be a 7 day challenge on how to do "x." For example, say you're launching a new fitness app you could call your challenge the "7-Day FitRipped Challenge" and each day you'll do a 20 minute Facebook live video about a topic or workout within the app where you ask people to follow along, then you show them the app you have in beta and ask them what features they'd like to see, try to respond right within the Live platform, and let them know that they will be able to get a VIP insider offer by attending the video. From there you boost your Live Video to your target audience and let them know a new video will be available the next day as part of the 7-day challenge at say 10 a.m. Where you'll cover the next topic. You can then use those videos and offer them up to a complementary business who has a list that is say about 5000-10000 people on their list (you won't be able to go after a big list if don't have anyone on yours yet). Your offer will be simple: Help me pre-launch my app and email your list my videos, and when I launch the app I'll send over a check for a referral fee on all items I sell as a result of your list buying my product. Keep in mind by the 7th day that's when you let them know that the cart will be open for them to buy the product but only for a limited time (2 days is typical). The key on each video is to ask all people attending to register online to be notified when the product is going to be available, so you will need to build a landing page with either LeadPages.net, unbounce.com, or OptimizePress, then link it to your email marketing solution (MailChimp, Aweber, etc), and your shopping cart (that could SamCart or something similar).

"Use your audience to help shape your product and make them feel like it's their own so they end up buying it and telling their friends."

If you do have a list, I'd recommend the same process but to your existing audience on email, social, and other channels you may have available to you. The key in the Pre-Launch phase is to think of it as the time where you give valuable content away, prime the prospect for your purchase, and then let them know when the cart will be open for purchase.

"The key in the Pre-Launch phase is to think of it as the time where you give valuable content away, prime the prospect for your purchase, and then let them know when the cart will be open for purchase."

After you have your list of subscribers you can start telling your story of the product, how it came to be, the science behind it, the social proof of the friends and family, and the results you could expect to see. A good framework and sequence to follow would be as follows:

Email 1: Thank you for your interest in Fitness App X
Email 2 (day 1): Why I created Fitness App X and how everything you know is wrong

* Tell your story on why you were frustrated with all fitness solutions out there that just don't work and how you stumbled onto the idea for your fitness app (the big problem it solves)

Email 3 (day 2): New Video today on X and How I knew I was on to a fitness breakthrough

* Continue to tell your story on how you started seeing results and why you started to make the app

Email 4 (day 3): New video today on X and How you will change your fitness forever in less time
Email 5 (day 4): new video today on X and why my friend x will never go to the gym again

* Social proof email where you story tell with testimonials

Email 6 (day 5): New video today on X and how the science of x changes everything
Email 7 (day 6): New video today on X and how the fitness app is like a personal trainer in your pocket

Email 8 (day 7): Last video today on X and what special insider secrets I'm sharing

* In this email you'll want to set up your offer that's coming in the launch phase. At this point your prospect is getting primed to hear what deal they'll get and how you can really help them with your big challenge (in this case their fitness level)

Phase 2: Launch Phase

In the launch phase you'll want to send a series of emails designed to really create a sense of urgency and scarcity that help convert your prospect to a sale, then you'll want to up-sell them to grow your basket size. It's critical to note that your goal when you structure your offers is to get a nice introductory offer for folks who don't really know you and don't have to set aside a big amount of money; typical ranges are $1-$39. Then an up-sell to $97, then $197, then $497 as examples. I think you get the idea – start off low and move them up your sales ladder (or sales funnel) with larger purchases.

Why would you do this? To increase your average order amount, so when put your paid media on you can pay more for the ads and still make money. Using our fitness app as an example you could offer the app for a $1.99 recurring fee monthly, then up-sell them to a $97 meal plan, then a $197 personalized workout plan designed by you, and then finally a $497 up-sell that includes personal phone calls, personalized workout plan, nutrition plan, and to be part of your VIP insider Facebook group.

"It's critical to note that your goal when you structure your offers is to get a nice introductory offer for folks who don't

really know you and don't have to set aside a big amount of money; typical ranges are $1-$39."

With your email series, you will want to use them to help guide your prospect to each step through the funnel. This is a typical email series to help do that...

Email 1 (3 days before launch): New Fitness App Coming in 3 days

* Tell them that there are great features, you took feedback, made it better, etc

Email 2 (2 days before launch): Insider Launch to a Select Few just 2 days away

* Tell them that there are only a limited group of people that are getting this launch and they are one of them

Email 3 (1 day before launch): Launch Day Tomorrow

* Look out for the email

Email 4 (Launch Day): It's here, Get the limited time offer

* Ideally on launch day you have the shopping cart open for a limited time at your offer deal (2 days as an example) and let your customer know that they have to act now or the launch deal is going away never to return. By using this traditional scarcity technique people will feel compelled to convert.

On your landing page have all the offer details on this limited time offer with a countdown clock, the science, the testimonials, and of course the big call to action. Once someone enters to buy the offer, hit them up with another offer on the second page of the site (this is your first up-sell we discussed earlier). If they decline or accept, then on the 3rd page up-sell them to the larger offer and then again on the 4th page to the largest most valuable offer. You'll have the highest conversion rate on offer 1, then 2, then 3, then 4. However, your average order amount will be higher using this 4-stage up-sell funnel because of the take rate from each offer, thus enabling your to add on the paid advertising to the top of the funnel or your first landing page.

> *"Once someone enters to buy the offer, hit them up with another offer on the second page of the site."*

What happens if someone doesn't convert? Email your list of people that didn't convert, and how do you know this? You can set the rules of the email list to the point of a prospect email list, then a customer email list. Once someone converts to a customer they move to the customer list and get emails after they purchase. If they don't, then you send a series of emails after the cart opens to take action and buy before the cart closes. I find that 2 emails a day is about best. If you're using paid advertising it's also best to activate retargeting on Google and Facebook to hit up prospects that have not converted to go back to the cart page to buy. After this phase you'll want to enter into your last phase of your product launch.

> *"Set the rules of the email list to the point of a prospect email list, then a customer email list. Once someone converts to a customer they move to the customer list and get emails after they purchase."*

Phase 3: Post-Launch

Now your offer is closed, you had your sales blitz, and you're done right? No, not exactly. Now it's time to email your customers and tell them what to do next. Once they become customers and are on your customer list it's your chance to ensure they are using your product, become satisfied, do reviews, and then become your advocates. Remember a current customer is the best customer to grow into a more valuable customer over time. For example your email series can look like this:

Email 1 (Day 1): Thanks for your purchase

  *   How to get started

Email 2 (Day 1): How to use Fitness App X for best results
Email 3 (Day 2): What people are saying about Fitness App X
Email 4 (Day 2): Write a review about Fitness App X
Email 5 (Day 3): Share Fitness App X and Get Y

  *   This email asks your existing customers to share an offer code you create with their friends so you can grow your customer base from existing customers (this is advocacy). Typically, people associate with like people within the same life stage and economic situation – so they are the most valuable asset you have.

With your different offers I suggest creating different email lists tied to each offer so you can customize your communication to each customer segment. This allows you to put in an up-sell every few email communications to get them up into the next more valuable customer segment, which makes you more money! This is the secret to CRM and the life-cycle management of customers.

"Put in an up-sell every few email communications to get them up into the next more valuable customer segment, which makes you more money!"

It also goes without saying that your website, whether you're using Infusionsoft or Leadpages with Drip and Samcart integrations you'll need to ensure your products they can use are on the sites, or apps, or can be ordered via the store. Furthermore, with a sales funnel automation strategy you should be able to close more leads and grow your customers, but I encourage you to experiment with the emails, landing pages, integrate membership or private Facebook groups to get more touch points and grow the affinity towards your brand just like a good salesperson or marketer does.

"Experiment with the emails, landing pages, integrate membership or private Facebook groups to get more touch points and grow the affinity towards your brand just like a good salesperson or marketer does."

In fact, sales automation done properly is like a full sales kennel all working together to close a deal. If you haven't heard of this, the concept of a sales kennel was popularized by Blair Singer, who consults for Robert Kiyosaki of *Rich Dad Poor Dad,* who explained salespeople are like dogs. For example, a Pitbull is your aggressive sales guy who is a great closer, but is horrible at follow up and follow through. Your paid ad is like a Pitbull that goes for the close right away. Then the follow up, follow through is the Golden Retriever sales person who is right there trying to add value, help you answer questions, and make you feel special during your buying process and post buying process. Then the product features explanation, science, and all technical stuff is what your Chihuahua is great at, and finally the Poodle is the sales person that everyone knows and is flashy, friendly, and looks like a million bucks. That Poodle is the aspiration you sell in your offers, the testimonials that you share, and the hope you sell. So you can see that the sales automation process actually emulates the perfect sales process you would have if you put all your sales associates with different skills together to help guide a prospect all the way through to a sale. Imagine if you had that kind of attention as a buyer? Would you buy? Damn straight, and that's why it's worth it to invest in your sales automation process and start making some serious scalable money. Get to it!

> *"The sales automation process actually emulates the perfect sales process you would have if you put all your sales associates with different skills together to help guide a prospect all the way through to a sale. Imagine if you had that kind of attention as a buyer?"*

Chapter 21

How to Set Up Amazon for Business Success

How can you talk about building businesses today without talking about Amazon? From an up and coming bookstore to a world-renowned e-commerce giant – Amazon has entirely changed the game of retail, media consumption, and fostered the adoption of the long-tail. Now they've entered nearly all categories, but more importantly are the primary search engine for products. In fact, according to an article on Reuters a couple years ago Amazon received over 30% of all search queries online for products and Google received 13%. After speaking to industry experts and even Amazon themselves that stat is over 50% now at the time of writing this book in 2017, for Amazon! The impact to retail commerce here is that of a tsunami.

> *"Amazon received over 30% of all search queries online for products and Google received 13%. After speaking to industry experts and even Amazon themselves that stat is over 50%... The impact to retail commerce here is that of a tsunami."*

Think about your own behavior; do you go to Google or Amazon to see it, read the description, see reviews, and look at alternatives? If you're like most you go to Amazon because it's easier to get the comparative info you want to justify your buying decision. Knowing this, Amazon launched an entire ecosystem to help entrepreneurs get their products in front of an Amazon consumer and every time you do as that entrepreneur they make money and hopefully you do too.

> *"If you're like most you go to Amazon because it's easier to get the comparative info you want to justify your buying decision."*

So how do you set your business on Amazon and make it scalable? Well there are two ways to accomplish this: Vendor Central or Seller Central.

Vendor Central

The Amazon model where you sell your goods to Amazon directly as a retailer. They buy your goods outright, issue a PO, and list them online. You of course will still have to provide them with content to populate your product pages and if want pages that convert, then you need to spring for A+ pages, Vine consumer reviews, and ads, so those will cost you. Additionally, they will ask you for trade dollars for promotions in the area of 12-15%, damages, allowances, returns, etc. If you don't conform to their operational processes strictly, you will also face penalties that can quickly add up. Furthermore, they will charge you a premium for Advanced Analytics to get to see who is buying your goods, how they get to your page, and what else they buy.

> *"Vendor Central is the Amazon model where you sell your goods to Amazon directly as a retailer... they will ask you for trade dollars for promotions in the area of 12-15%, damages, allowances, returns."*

The benefit to Vendor Central is consumers tend to trust Amazon as a seller more than outside parties. The biggest issue with Vendor Central is pricing! If you decide to list with Amazon under Vendor Central give them a price that won't hurt your other channels because Amazon has a search algorithm that matches the lowest price for the same item online to then acquire customers. This can lead to channel conflict if you're not careful. A fix for this is to list a different size product or variation with a different UPC code to help avoid that conflict. For example, if you have a product on Walmart at $9.99 with 30 servings and feature A, then make new items at $9.99 with 29 servings and feature B. That way Walmart will be happy and you will still win on Amazon. Ultimately, if you're starting out Vendor should not be your best option because it could cost you if you're not careful.

> *"Amazon has a search algorithm that matches the lowest price for the same item online to then acquire customers. This can lead to channel conflict if you're not careful."*

Seller Central

This is the best if you're a smaller business and want to grow your business with Amazon as a viable channel before entering into Vendor Central. You can sign up as an individual seller or a professional seller. Individual seller accounts are roughly $40 a month with around a 100 units a month in sales. If you do volume above that then a Professional seller account is right for you and Amazon waves the monthly fee, but takes a percentage of sales from you – on average that's about 15%. You also have the option of using your own fulfillment center with the Professional seller account, if you are able to meet the Amazon ship by requirements.

"Seller Central is best if you're a smaller business and want to grow your business with Amazon as a viable channel before entering into Vendor Central."

Amazon also offers distribution for you with a service called FBA or Fulfillment By Amazon. The big advantage to this service is it allows you to offer free shipping to consumers on Amazon and to Prime eligible as well. Prime consumers buy more often and spend more than non-Prime members, so you definitely want to reach those consumers. Remember Prime members pay $99/yr to be Prime members and thus usually only search for Prime eligible products to be able to get their 2-day free shipping.

"Prime consumers buy more often and spend more than non-Prime members."

The fees associated to Amazon FBA are pick, pack and handling fees, warehousing fee based on weights, size, etc. The best way to see the costs for you using FBA is searching for the Amazon FBA calculator on Google to get the most recent one. It will break down all recent costs for you vs your existing fulfillment. Oh, and another benefit to using FBA is that Amazon will handle all customer service and chargebacks/returns. This allows you to focus on what's most important to you – sales and marketing.

What most people don't know is that you can use FBA as your primary distribution/fulfillment center with your own e-commerce store. Say for example you use Shopify as your store, you can integrate with FBA and then pay a $5 multi-channel fee (usually the cost of the shipping) to cover the cost of the service. So if you set up your Amazon store and your own e-commerce store you can now run all inventory through one fulfillment center and streamline your operations. However, if you chose to use another fulfillment center that is, say, more direct response oriented, here is a good list of folks I've either worked with or had colleagues recommend:

Fosdick Fulfillment
Innotrac
Moulton
Efulfillment
DataPak

Now, this sounds great, but what do I sell? If that's what you're asking yourself right now then you can use some tools to find the white space in the marketplace so you can increase your chance at succeeding. First go to Amazon.com and type "best sellers" in the search bar to see the top 100 best sellers on Amazon. That will give you the quick view of what is hot on Amazon and where to look for trends. If that's too much info for you, drill down by category and look at the sales rank, number of reviews, star ratings, and insights in the reviews. Do folks keep on talking about something bad about the best-selling product? If so, that might be an area to attack and monetize the white space. You can also use tools like SellerLabs.com to pay for research on what sells on Amazon.

> *"Go to Amazon.com and type "best sellers" in the search bar to see the top 100 best sellers on Amazon. That will give you the quick view of what is hot on Amazon and where to look for trends."*

What about reselling versus creating your own brand? You can do either with Amazon, but it's recommended to build your own brand if you can to differentiate against the competition. Reselling usually comes down to price and getting as much margin as you can is where you want to live. Margin fixes all mistakes and if you are operating on thin margins as a reseller you must first master the Amazon platform. However, if you're hell bent on looking at reselling then go to alibaba.com to see if you can find a supplier. Alibaba is a Chinese trade exchange where suppliers list their raw materials or finished goods where sales and marketing firms can source their goods. Depending on your industry you can use the Thompson Registry to find manufacturers.

What about your label? Check out 99designs.com or designcrowd. com to get designers to quote on your design brief, then have friends or families vote on the best design. It could cost you anywhere from $199 to $499 depending on the scope of the project. Still much cheaper than working with a dedicated freelancer who may be bogged down with another project or only have one design specialty.

> *"Alibaba is a Chinese trade exchange where suppliers list their raw materials or finished goods where sales and marketing firms can source their goods. Depending on your industry you can use the Thompson Registry to find manufacturers."*

How do you price your products on Amazon? We did discuss fees that Amazon has, so you'll want to cover those costs and a rule of thumb is to have at least 3-5 times markup to cover your costs and have some profit left over (about $15 margin if you can). On direct response items I usually look for 5-8 times markup, so if you can price higher and be competitive or unique enough to do so, do it! Like I said earlier – margin fixes mistakes.

> *"Rule of thumb is to have at least 3-5 times markup to cover your costs and have some profit left over (about $15 margin if you can)."*

How do you get your product promoted to gain trial? You may not want to hear this, but you'll have to give it away to drive trial. The best way is to do a Facebook ad, drive to a lead page (leadpages.com is a good tool), put in an offer that says "company X wants you to try a new product just released" in the ad, then to the landing page with the offer at a value just enough to cover your cost of goods, have a coupon code associated to the offer that you generated in Professional seller account, ask for that code in exchange for the coupon (hint: get testimonials on your landing page by giving your product away to seeders like friends and family so they can give you reviews you can put on your page to help conversions), then ask your new prospect to buy the product on amazon (link to your product page from the coupon thank you page), then ask your prospect in an email to write a review after they receive the product (remember you captured the email address) about 3-5 days later.

Expert tip: Use a 5 day email sequence and value adds to build a relationship with the consumer to the review is likely to get posted. Think of this as priming up your customer with kindness so they can give you some love back. Furthermore, you'll fly up the sales rankings doing this because Amazon's algorithm rewards conversion rates; the higher the conversion rate, the better your sales rank. Once you get your rankings up higher, more reviews show up, and natural sales start coming in you can stop the ad sequence and make your profits. Think of this phase as your rapid growth investment phase.

> *"How do you get your product promoted to gain trial? You may not want to hear this, but you'll have to give it away to drive trial. The best way is to do a Facebook ad and drive to a lead page."*

Note: Did you notice that we're collecting email addresses while we are selling on Amazon? We are because now the next time you launch a product you can email your customers and have sales right out of the gate. You can even drive them to your own store and make more profit. Remember, the guy with the largest list wins. That's why Dollar Shave

Club sold to Unilever for a billion dollars. Additionally, rule of thumb is that you should be making about $1 in sales for every name in your database, so the faster you get up to a million names, the faster you get to be a millionaire.

> *"You should be making about $1 in sales for every name in your database, so the faster you get up to a million names, the faster you get to be a millionaire."*

Another important thing to remember when advertising your products is to have the right email marketing service that delivers the coupon code and the sequence of emails listed above. Again, you can use MailChimp, Aweber, Drip, etc. Whatever you choose, your email sequence should be over 5 days and contain these emails:

Day 1: Thank you here's you coupon
Day 2: My story and why this exists
Day 3: The science of the product or cool features
Day 4: Social Proof

* what people are saying and why they love my product

Day 5: CTA

* why haven't you used my coupon? it expires soon
* here's you want to ask them to refer this to their friend too and use scarcity

Post Purchase Bonus Email Sequence:

To help get more reviews use your email service to have another two emails generated and sent 7 days after your first email to both ask for a review on Amazon and to also recommend your product to a friend.

Day 7: Did you like Product X? Leave a Review
Day 8: Spread the word on Product X

* get creative, maybe even give another coupon to the customer for the referral

If you're not sure if the customer actually bought and you won't be you can use a took called Feedback Five (feedbackfive.com). You can automatically send emails to customers who bought your products on Amazon and it's a set it and forget approach. This can eliminate the need for the post-purchase email sequence I mapped out above.

Other tools you can use are AMS (Amazon Media Services) to do sponsored keyword ads within the Amazon marketplace to drive traffic to your page. You can create the ads right within the Amazon portal. The ad tool works on a cost per click model and can be profitable if the cost is right and your margins are high enough. I suggest using it after the Facebook model discussed above.

"You can use a took called Feedback Five. You can automatically send emails to customers who bought your products on Amazon."

What about taxes? If you're an international vendor and do business with Amazon USA, just make sure you fill out the proper W8-BEN forms and remit your taxes. You may want to discuss this with a tax advisor and there are forums within Amazon that can help you avoid any pitfalls that can stall your business.

> *"If you're an international vendor and do business with Amazon USA, just make sure you fill out the proper W8-BEN forms and remit your taxes."*

Now you're informed with how to go to market with Amazon and whether it's your primary channel or a secondary channel done properly it can become quite lucrative. The biggest thing I would ask you is that if you're not on Amazon, get on there and going! The retail environment is changing and if you're not selling online you may be extinct in several years.

Final Thoughts

I truly believe that this books holds valuable tips and strategies that can help make you more money as an entrepreneur, business owner, shareholder, or even in your career as a marketer. More importantly, I hope you have some affirmation on some things you've had a hunch on or wanted to try for a while now but have yet to act. The one thing I will say is most important is to actually ACT! Yes, take action, learn, fire bullets before you fire cannonballs, and don't let fear guide your actions. No one follows the scared, they follow the bold, the brave, the believers! It's time to act and start building your future.

I'd like to help build it with you and that's why I'm offering you an opportunity to join my *Marketing Genius Mastermind* group at themarketers commute.com/mastermind. There you'll meet some of the sharpest minds in the industry and you'll have access to me weekly where I'll be sharing strategies to help grow your business. Looking forward to seeing you there.

Yours truly,

Darren "I want you to kick ass at marketing" Contardo
DarrenContardo.net / TheMarketersCommute.com
@darrencontardo

For more book info and support materials visit marketingthatreallyworks.net

Darren C. Contardo, a husband and the father of two boys, has been in the marketing industry for twenty-two years. He holds a business degree and a postgraduate degree in e-commerce and entrepreneurship. At the beginning of his career, Contardo cofounded a company that provided privacy and security solutions for dot-com retailers.

He has built more than ten top-selling brands in the consumer packaged goods, nutrition, and health-and-wellness industries, with distribution in large retailers across North America, including SlimFast. Currently, Contardo is working in private equity in Palm Beach Gardens, Florida, where he resides. He also hosts *The Marketer's Commute*, a podcast in which he discusses his experience and offers marketing strategies.

www.ingramcontent.com/pod-product-compliance
Lightning Source LLC
Chambersburg PA
CBHW071537200326
41519CB00021BB/6512